"Vestigial Organs" Are Fully Functional

(A History and Evaluation of The Vestigial Organ Origins Concept)

by

Jerry Bergman, Ph.D. and George Howe, Ph.D.

With a foreword by David Menton, Ph.D.
of the Washington University School of Medicine
and a preface by V. Wright, M.D., F.R.C.P.,
of the University of Leeds

Creation Research Society
Monograph Series: No. 4

Creation Research Society Books
P.O. Box 8263
St. Joseph, MO 64508-8263

"Vestigial Organs" Are Fully Functional
by Jerry Bergman, Ph.D.
and George F. Howe, Ph.D.
Edited by Emmett L. Williams
Cover Design by Ross Marshall

ISBN: 0-940384-09-4

© 1990 Creation Research Society
All rights reserved. No part of this book may be reproduced in any form or by any means without permission in writing from the publisher.

Second Printing – May 1993
Third Printing – February 2003

Printed in the United States of America

TABLE OF CONTENTS

Topic	Page
A Foreword by Dr. David Menton	vii
A Preface by Dr. V. Wright	ix
INTRODUCTION	x

PART I: GENERAL DISCUSSION OF THE VESTIGIAL ORGAN CONCEPT

Definitions and Evolutionary Claims	1
Examples of Supposed Vestigial Organs	3
Rudimentary Organs Versus Vestigial Organs	4
Darwin and Wiedersheim on Vestigial Organs	5
Historical Importance of Vestigial Organs as "Proof" of Macroevolution and as a Serious "Problem" for Creationists	6
Surveys of Vestigial Organ Discussions in Textbooks	9
Is the Vestigial Organ Controversy a "Dead Horse?"	10
The Vestigial Organ Concept as an Evidence Against The Belief in Design	11
Dysteleology—An Evolutionary Theology	11
Does The Vestigial Organ Argument Stifle Research?	12
Four Types of So-Called Vestigial Organs	13
Functions Found for "Useless" Organs	13
It Would Be Difficult to Prove That an Organ is Functionless	15
If A Structure Were Really Useless, Would It Be Expected to Disappear?	15
Does Evolutionism Lead to Self-Contradictory Predictions Regarding Vestigial Organs?	16
Do Vestigial Organs "Prove Too Much?"	17
Vestigial Organ Discussions in the Popular Media— Lamarackian Philosophy Still Runs Rampant	17
The Loss Mutation View of Vestigial Organ Origin	19
Do Homeotic Mutations Help Explain The Origin of New Organs?	20
Negative Allometry and Vestigial Organs	20
Panmixia and Reversal of Selection as Explanations for Vanishing Vestigial Organs	20
The "Law" of Material Compensation and Vestigial Organs	21
Some of The So-Called Vestigial Organs May Result from a Developmental Plan	22
Coding Theory and Organs Labeled "Vestigial"	23
Were All Code Packages Designed at One Time?	26

The Decay Principle and
    Some Putative Vestigial Organs 27
The Concept of Overdesign 27
Homology and Aphanisia 29
The Problem of Purpose 30
The Lack of Nascent Organs Is a Problem to
    Macroevolutionists 31
Vestigial Organs as a Test of Origins Predictions 31

PART II: FUNCTIONS OF SPECIFIC ORGANS STILL BELIEVED TO BE USELESS VESTIGES

The Coccyx Defined as a Supposed Vestige.................... 32
Contributions of the Coccyx 32
Does the Human Embryo Have a Tail? 34
Are Some Human Babies Actually Born with a Tail? 35
The Tonsils and Adenoids Described 37
The Vestigial Label and Tonsil Surgery 37
Tonsil Functions Now Known 39
A Description of the Vermiform Appendix..................... 39
Problems with the Appendix 40
The Taxonomic Distribution of Appendices
    Confounds Phylogeny 41
The Cecum, Cellulose, and the Appendix...................... 42
The Appendix, Antibodies, and Post-Radiation Survival 43
The Appendix Has Lymphatic Functions 44
A Possible Tie Between Cancer and the
    Absence of the Appendix 45
Appendectomies and Origins 46
The Thymus... 47
Description of the Thymus.................................... 48
Functions of the Thymus...................................... 48
Description of the Pineal Gland—
    Another Supposed Vestigial Organ 49
Light Is Shed on the Pineal Gland's Functions 50
The Pineal Gland and Melatonin Production 51
Circadian Rhythms and Pineal Gland Activity.................. 53
The "Nictitating Membrane" in the Human Eye—
    The Plica Similunaris 55
The Eyebrows and Eyelashes Were Once
    Considered Vestigial..................................... 57
The Ear Muscles 58
Darwin's Point on the Ear 58
The Mammae, Nipples, and Areolae in Human Males.......... 59
Male Nipples and Embryological Design 60

iv

Extra Nipples and Mammary Glands in Strange Places 61
What About the Yolk Sac in Humans? 61
Is the Human Pharynx Badly Designed? 62
Are Human "Goose Pimples" and Body Hair Vestigial.......... 63
Is Human Body Hair Useless? 64
Muscle and Bone Variations as Vestigial Organs 66
Wisdom Teeth or Third Molars 67
Are Spurs on Snakes Vestigial 69
The Hip Bones of the Whale 70
The Fossil Record of Whales 71
The Leg Bones of Whales 73
Teeth in the Whale Fetus 74
The Horse Splint Bones 77
Blind Cave Creatures 77
Explanations for Cave Blindness 79
Are There Vestigial Organs in Plants? 82
A Guidance Chemical for Pollen Tubes 83
In Conclusion 84
REFERENCES 86

A Foreword by David Menton, Ph.D.
Associate Professor of Anatomy
Department of Anatomy and Neurobiology
Washington University School of Medicine
St. Louis, Missouri

The American College Dictionary gives the definition of a biological vestige as a ". . . degenerate or imperfectly developed organ or structure having little or no utility, but which in an earlier stage performed a useful function." From the time of Darwin, it has been assumed by scientists that all animals and plants should show numerous examples of "vestigial organs" or remnants of their evolutionary history. Assuming that neo-Darwinian evolution is a fact, the only requirement for the vestigial status of any organ is that it be considered largely non-functional or without known function. Since ignorance of the function of any organ would clearly favor its being classed as "vestigial," it is not surprising that the list of vestigial organs has greatly decreased with increasing knowledge and scientific study. Still, the concept of vestiges, together with the closely related concept of homology, continue to be cited as evidence in support of classical neo-Darwinian evolution. These old and often discredited ideas are currently enjoying a resurgence in the guise of modern molecular biology. We thus occasionally see references to vestigial and homologous proteins, but the basis of the argument remains the same and still raises the same questions.

As to the related question of homologous organs, what exactly does it indicate if two different organisms have nearly identical organs or proteins? What can we conclude if both striking similarities and differences are found between two different organisms? How consistent are we in interpreting the putative evolutionary significance of similarities or differences between different organisms? What, for example, is the evolutionary significance or homologous or vestigial organs when striking similarities between otherwise unrelated organisms, such as the eyes of octopi and mammals, can be glibly dismissed as "convergent evolution?" Should we consider the rudimental mammary glands of males as homologous or vestigial organs?

Professors Jerry Bergman and George Howe have attempted to address those and other questions in this book, but their answers may not please those with a predetermined mindset on origins. Many scientists assume *a priori* that all observations must be consistent, even if they are forced. It will be obvious to the reader that Drs. Bergman and Howe do not begin with the usual assumption of classical neo-Darwinian evolution. The reader who can deal with such heresy will find this criticism of the vestigial organ paradigm most thought-provoking.

A Preface by V. Wright, M.D., F.R.C.P.
Professor of Rheumatology
University of Leeds, U.K.

Darwinian evolution has suffered badly at the hands of paleontology in recent days. The virtual absence of transitional forms in the fossil records is so clear that on the anniversary of Darwin's death the London Times published a scathing attack on the model. It was accompanied by a cartoon showing the great man, clutching a book entitled "The Descent of Man," slipping up on a banana skin surreptitiously placed under his foot by a monkey slinking away in the corner of the picture. The moment paleontologists begin to talk about punctuated equilibria, they are only a step away from a creation model.

Another plank at one time thought to be firm in the evolutionary platform was that of vestigial organs. Many biologists have discarded this view, yet several protagonists persist in citing them as evidence. In this comprehensive, closely argued volume, Dr. Bergman and Dr. Howe show how facile is that view. Their treatise ranges from the appendix to the thymus, from male nipples to wisdom teeth, and from the coccyx to the parathyroids. Researchers have now shown that structures which were dismissed as inconsequential have an important role to play. Indeed, with a gland such as the thymus the function has been shown to be crucial to the immunological defense of the body.

These matters are not merely academic—important though truth for truth's sake is. In my own field of rheumatology we did not believe the frequently quoted old wives' tale that man suffered from backache because he has assumed an upright position. We have shown that quadrupeds are subject to slipped discs as frequently as man, and often with disastrous results. Similarly, the menisci of the knee were dismissed as being of little consequence. Our own work has shown that they bear up to 80% of the load in certain phases of walking, that their damage predisposes to osteoarthritis of the knee, and a modification of the removal of the organ under certain circumstances is desirable.

None would doubt the microevolution of a species, whether by deliberate selective breeding or by environmental changes, but at the end of the day a cow is still a cow, a peppered moth is still a peppered moth, and a finch is still a finch. The leap in logic to macroevolution has little supportive evidence. This book makes a positive contribution in showing the function of organs once dismissed as vestigial.

INTRODUCTION

Macroevolutionists have asserted that when organisms evolved, certain organs lost part or all of their functions. These "vestigial organs" in plants, animals, and humans are structures that are believed to have had some function in the past, but are no longer needed and no longer functional as a result of the evolutionary changes. Some macroevolutionists believe that these changes were caused by natural selection of gene mutations (neo-Darwinism) while others imagine that sweeping changes occurred rapidly at various intervals throughout geologic history (the punctuated equilibrium concept).

Vestigial organs are supposed to be somewhat like old computers that have been replaced by newer models with greater speed and more efficient design. But the body cannot easily "drop parts" as a computer designer can, and in the macroevolutionist's view these vestigial organs are leftover components that were once important, but are now merely remnants of their previous identity.

Until very recently, vestigial organs were interpreted to be strong evidence favoring macroevolution. The vestigial organ argument was considered one of the strongest supporting data of evolution for well over a century. But of the approximately 180 vestigial organs compiled by researchers around the year 1900, it is now almost unanimously agreed that most of them have at least one function in the body. After examining the few organs still generally believed to be vestigial, it can be concluded that each of these also has one or more functions.

The tonsils, adenoids, coccyx, nictitating membrane, pineal gland, and thymus gland were examples of putative vestigial organs. Researchers have found that most of these so-called vestigial organs played several roles. Some are back-up organs, operative in unusual situations or during only certain stages of the organism's life. Such information has been very slow to find its way into the textbooks of biology and origins. For example, several major functions of the so-called nictitating membrane in the eye were delineated in the 1920's, yet some science text writers still label this organ "vestigial." Researchers continue to find additional functions for other organs once deemed vestigial.

Discussion of supposedly vestigial organs as evidence for evolution is not merely abstract philosophy but has practical medical implications. The belief in vestigial organs had discouraged research on the function of many body organs and had encouraged certain medical practices which are now regrettable.

The appendix was seen as worse than useless, a likely site of infection; as such, it was subject to removal as soon as possible. It is now believed by many scientists that the appendix serves an important role in the body's immune defense system.

There are other examples of unfortunate surgical procedures spawned by the evolutionary vestigial organ argument. It was once a common practice to remove the tonsils and adenoids, both of which are now known to be immunologically important organs, especially in young persons.

Since medical research has all but closed the door to consideration of organs in the human body as "functionless," some macroevolutionists still assert that there are useless organs in the bodies of such animals as whales, pythons, and horses. Although our primary emphasis here concerns human organs, we shall discuss several supposed vestiges in various animals and one in plants.

The authors have been evaluating the problem of vestigial organs for many years. Bergman had his first exposure to the concept of supposed vestigial organs at age five. A family physician, observing young Bergman's practice of mouth-breathing, recommended removal of both the tonsils and adenoids, partially because, as the doctor put it, "It is better to have them out now when you are young than when you are older." Asked why they needed to be removed, the doctor answered, "They have no use and should come out as soon as possible."

Fascinated, Bergman asked what must be the usual questions concerning how the tonsils got there and what their function is. The doctor's only reply, that one is ". . . born with them, but they are useless," was baffling and five-year-old Bergman could not understand why a person would have a useless organ.

Now we know that the tonsils are useful and should not be removed until all other remedies are tried. Researchers have found that people who have had tonsillectomies, for example, are four times more likely to develop Hodgkin's disease than those with tonsils—see Galton (1976:26-27).

Extensive reading and discussion with colleagues has led us to conclude that every organ labeled "useless" is not functionless. Ignorance alone has prevented scientists from understanding these organs. We feel confident that future research will eliminate the few remaining structures from the "vestigial" organ category.

In this present work we center primarily on the history of science because most of the conclusions herein are now generally accepted by the authorities in the various medical and biological specialties, no matter what philosophy of origins they hold. Our task was to review the literature and to tie together various sectors of vestigial organ research. We have relied heavily upon work reported in medical or scientific journals and on the conclusions made by the researchers themselves.

The amount of literature is enormous; we have unearthed dozens of articles and six books on the pineal gland alone. In our extensive study, however, we were not able to locate a single book or monograph published in English this century covering all the vestigial organs, although numerous reviews have been produced on specific organs. It is our hope that this book will fill a void in the current origins literature.

Accomplishing the research for a monograph like this one often takes many years and involves the help and cooperation of scores of individual scientists. This work is no exception. We are grateful for the help of many people who aided in this work, especially Dr. Margaret Falding, Dept. of Biomedical Sciences, University of Guelph, Ontario, Canada; Dr. David Menton, Dept. of Anatomy, Washington University of Medicine; Dr. John King, Dept. of Ophthalmology, Ohio State University, Columbus, Ohio; Dr. John Meyer, formerly of the School of Medicine, University of Louisville and presently with Baptist Bible College, Clarks Summit, Pennsylvania, and Mr. Thomas Pittman.

Although the authors take sole responsibility for the content of these pages, we thank the members of the Creation Research Society Publications and Monograph Committees for authorizing this project and for submitting valuable suggestions on its revision. We express special thanks to the following members of the Creation Research Society Board for their help in improving the manuscript: Dr. Wayne Frair, Dr. Wilbert Rusch, Sr., Dr. Emmett Williams, and Dr. Glenn Wolfrom. We also thank Mrs. Phyllis Hughes for able assistance in preparing the manuscript. We are indebted to Ms. Lazella Lawson and Ms. Beth Howe for help in the library search phases of this study. We thank the publishers of *Origins Research* (Colorado Springs) for permission to quote extensively from their journal and the editors of Dehoff Publications (Murfreesboro, TN) for permission to reproduce lengthy quotations from Douglas Dewar's book, *The Transformist Illusion*.

Jerry Bergman, Ph.D. and
George F. Howe, Ph.D.

PART 1: GENERAL DISCUSSION OF THE VESTIGIAL ORGAN CONCEPT

Definitions and Evolutionary Claims

Macroevolutionism, which is sometimes called megaevolutionism, is the belief that major changes have occurred in the bodies of organisms, over long periods of time, resulting in new, living types that are most successfully adapted to a changing environment. Most macroevolutionists assume that all living forms are branches of only one or very few "ancestral trees."

Microevolutionism, on the other hand, is the study of minor variations usually occurring within the boundaries of one species or leading to the origin of two or more new species from one older species. Although most microevolution is hypothetical and unverifiable, some scientific evidences such as mutations, "race rings," and fluctuations of gene frequencies in gene pools support limited microevolutionary change. The support for macroevolution, however, lies entirely outside the boundaries of empirical science.

Scientists have been spectacularly unsuccessful in showing the origin of any major living types by means of field or laboratory experimentation. Furthermore, microevolution has not been shown to lead to or cause macroevolution even if vast periods of time are involved. The best that macroevolutionists have been able to show is that their origins view seem to "fit" with certain data from biology. Vestigial organs are among those items which macroevolutionists claim as support for their origins model and for their model only.

Historically, vestigial organs were considered one of the most important of the evidences demanding megaevolution. These supposedly useless organs are body structures which were believed to have served some function at one time in an organism's history; now they are no longer functional; see Heinze (1973). Drummond has asserted that vestigial organs favor evolution and only evolution by proposing that they are:

> ... actual betrayals ... veritable physical survivals, the material scaffolding ... of the [human] animal past ... so the body of Man, emerging from its age-long journey through the animal kingdom, appears laden with the spoils of its distant pilgrimage. These relics are not mere curiosities ... they were once a part of life's vicissitude; they represent organs which have been outgrown; old forms of apparatus long since exchanged for better, yet somehow not yet destroyed by the hand of time. The physical body of Man, so great is the number of these relics, is ... a museum of obsolete anatomies, discarded tools, outgrown and aborted organs. All other animals also contain among their useful organs a proportion which are long past their work; and so significant are these rudiments of a former state of things, that *anatomists have often expressed their willing-*

ness to stake the theory of Evolution upon their presence alone. [emphasis ours]. Drummond (1903:82-83)

In a leading and now classic college biology book, the well-known Alfred Kinsey (famous for his 1940's research on human sexual behavior) expressed the opinion that vestigial organs are a testimony to evolution just as many English words have remnants that show their Latin derivation. He stated that an important proof of evolution:

> ... is the collection of small and useless structures which are always to be found in species. Vestiges we call them. They appear to be remnants of things that were well developed and had some use among the ancestral organisms, but which have now almost disappeared in more developed forms. . . . Vestiges are similar to the G's in such English words as *reign* and *sign*. The latter is not pronounced in those words, and is now useless, but it is positive evidence of their origin from the older Latin words, *regnum* and *signum*. Kinsey (1920:200-201).

A. Thomson argued that humans have so many vestigial organs that the human ". . . body swarms with relics . . ." of the past. After listing those which he believed to be vestigial, A. Thomson concluded that:

> In our body we carry about several scores of useless relics which tell us some things about the past. Their persistence shows us that the past lives on within us, even in trivialities. But many of these vestiges are little details which are unfamiliar [to most people] except to the anatomist. A. Thomson (1958:203)

Like A. Thomson, most evolutionists define a vestigial organ as being useless. Crapo, however, and some other evolutionists, argued that if any organ formerly served some *other* function than it does now, it should be called "vestigial":

> This is precisely how a vestige should be defined: not as a 'functionless' part of an organism, but as a part which does not function in the way that its structure would lead us to expect, given how that structure functions in most other organisms. It is the fact that the baleen fetal 'teeth' are teeth *structurally* but *not functionally*, that makes them best defined as vestiges, and it is the existence of such vestiges in living organisms which evolutionary theory would very naturally predict, but which the belief in an efficient Designer would not lead us to expect *a priori*. Crapo (1985:1)

According to the evolutionary view of Crapo, *all* organs and body structures could be labeled "vestigial" because they have all changed their function during the theoretical eons of macroevolutionary history. In line with this definition, Crapo has even allowed that vestigial organs may have "functions" because the loss or change of any organ would have some "effect" on the rest of the system. Hence anything that could be called a "function" would be viewed by Crapo and those who adopt this definition as merely an "effect" of the reabsorption of the vestigial organ upon other parts of the system.

There is little to commend Crapo's revised definition of vestigial organs, except to macroevolutionists who might use it to escape the fact that organs once believed to be useless do in fact have functions. By redefining vestigial organs as those that have merely changed function, Crapo has created a failsafe bastion into which macroevolutionists may retreat when functions are found for other organs originally termed "useless." Yablokov (1974:233) has noted that part of the confusion surrounding the whole vestigial organ discussion arises from the fact that ". . . the vague or imprecise understanding of the vestigial organ concept present in the works of Darwin, persists to the present day."

The tactics of evolutionists like Crapo in dealing with and defining vestigial organs illustrate the non-falsifiable character of macroevolutionism. At first most macroevolutionists predicted that macroevolution ought to have produced organs that are totally without function. After physiologists had shown that most, if not all, of these supposedly useless organs have functions, the evolutionists then began to say that macroevolution would never have been expected to produce organs *without* functions, only organs with *changed* functions. R. Harris summarized the nonfalsifiable character of macroevolutionism as follows:

> When the evolutionist's first attack fails—'Hairs or appendixes are vestigial'—because we show him they have purpose or function, he reverts to the second argument or assertion, 'Ah yes, so that's why evolution preserved them.' R. Harris (1982:10)

Examples of Supposed Vestigial Organs

The most common example of a vestigial organ presented in both the scientific and popular literature on macroevolution is the human *vermiform appendix*—see Dodson and Dodson, (1976:49). Evolutionists concluded that when the human diet consisted of a higher proportion of cellulose plant material, the appendix was larger and provided an expanded chamber for the colonic digestion of roughage. They believed that the appendix then shrank in response to the modern human diet. Their tacit inference is that "disuse" is able to cause an organ to decrease in size and perhaps eventually disappear from the genotype, an assumption for which there is little or no empirical evidence.

Aside from the appendix, a few of the other commonly cited examples of vestigial organs are the human fifth toe (often called the "little toe," "small digit," or "fifth phalanx"); wisdom teeth ("third molars"); nipples on males; the mislabeled "nictitating membrane" in the human eye; the parathyroid, thymus, and pineal glands; and the caudal vertebrae or coccyx—see Rusch (1970:334-336) for a discussion of certain supposed vestigial organs.

Some evolutionists have strained to identify additional examples of vestigial organs—see Merrell (1962:101). The nodes on the ears, called "Darwin's tubercles" or "Darwin's points" are thought to be vestiges of our ancestors' ears which some evolutionists believe to have been larger and more pointed than our own—see Baitsell (1929:221). The muscles which enable some people to wiggle their outer ears are sometimes labeled vestigial and are assumed to have remained from a bygone period when directional hearing was an important means for man's ancestors to escape predation or to capture prey. Some animals can move their outer ears in the direction of the noise to detect more sound waves and thereby improve the loudness and quality of sounds. It is assumed that man's ancestors also possessed this capability.

Even some forms of human behavior are thought to be vestigial, such as the alleged "limb grasping" reflex which occurs when one scratches the instep of the bare foot. The tendency to swing one's arms while walking is imagined to be behavior which reveals our quadrupedal ancestry.

Rudimentary Organs Versus Vestigial Organs

One definition of the term "vestigial" provided by Kent (1978:435) is as follows: "A phylogenetic remnant that was better developed in an ancestor." Examples she included are the pelvic girdle of whales and the yolk sac of mammalian embryos. She classified as being "rudimentary" (as opposed to vestigial): ". . . structures that were more fully exploited in descendants" and thus were rudimentary in the phylogenic ancestor. She used the lagena of the fish inner ear (believed to be a rudimentary cochlea) as an example. Kent admitted, however, " . . . that it is not always possible to be certain whether a structure should be called rudimentary or vestigial." This is tantamount to an admission that from the vantage of macroevolutionism it is difficult to tell whether certain small organs are "coming or going." Such subjectivity demonstrates that macroevolutionism is not pure science but is an origins model based on one's personal philosophy.

Some researchers, such as Lull, distinguished vestigial organs from rudimentary structures by asserting that vestigial organs are supposedly in the process of "de-evolving." Vestigial organs are becoming retrogressive in development or tending toward diminution and ultimate loss; rudimentary organs are in " . . . the process of evolutionary growth and thus are progressing," according to Lull (1932:102). He cited as an example of a rudimentary organ certain animal horns which he assumed are now evolving to become more prominent than they were in fossil animals. As another example of vestigial organs, Lull cited horse leg bones:

> . . . the splints on either side of the cannon bone of a horse's foot [which] are vestiges of formerly useful lateral toes. Lull (1932:102).

Both examples are now recognized to be problematic, as we shall demonstrate.

Darwin and Wiedersheim on Vestigial Organs

Charles Darwin viewed vestigial organs as a major support for his thesis that microevolution by natural selection working on variations produces macroevolution over long periods of time. What we now call "vestigial organs" Darwin called "rudimentary organs" and discussed them extensively in the first chapter of his book, *The Descent of Man.* Darwin concluded that vestigial organs speak " . . . infallibly with respect to the nature of long lost structures."

This view that vestigial organs are evidence only for macroevolution was further developed by the German anatomist Wiedersheim (1895) who made it his life's work. As Scadding noted, Wiedersheim's development of the vestigial organ argument went well beyond Darwin's:

> . . . the identification of vestigial organs, especially in humans, reached a zenith in the work of the German anatomist, Wiedersheim . . . the discussion of vestigial organs in many biology textbooks owes more to Wiedersheim than to Darwin. In 'The Structure of Man,' Wiedersheim (1895) attempts to analyze human anatomy in evolutionary terms. Scadding (1983:5)

It was Wiedersheim (1895) who compiled a list of more than 180 rudimentary structures in man (86 vestigial and about 100 so-called retrogressive organs). One hundred and ten of the vestigial organs Wiedersheim recorded have a widespread distribution in man's body, according to Jordan and Kellogg, and:

> . . . occur in all the systems of organs, integument, skeleton, muscles, nervous system, sense organs, digestive, respiratory, circulatory and urino-genital systems. Most of these remnants of [past physical] structures are to be found completely developed in other vertebrate groups. Jordan and Kellogg (1908:175)

Wiedersheim's work on vestigial organs is an extremely impressive book containing a great deal of information on embryology, anatomy and physiology. He discussed many of the issues covered in this present work, including atavisms, the human tail, and polymasty.

Wiedersheim claimed that creationists cannot explain vestigial organ data, arguing that these organs:

> . . . which remain inexplicably by the doctrine of special creation or upon any teleological hypothesis can be satisfactorily explained by the theory of [natural] selection. Wiedersheim (1895:3)

Much of the groundwork for Wiedersheim was presented in Darwin's famous work *Origins of Species* in which he asserted that vestigial organs conflict with creation but support evolution:

> Organs or parts in this strange condition [vestigial] bearing the plain stamp of mutility, are extremely common . . . throughout would be impossible to name one of the higher animals in

which some part or other is not in a rudimentary condition . . . In reflecting on [vestigial organs] . . . the same reasoning power which tells us that most parts and organs are exquisitely adapted for certain purposes, tells us with equal plainness that these rudimentary or atrophied organs are imperfect and useless . . . rudimentary organs are generally said [by creationists] to have been created 'for the sake of symmetry,' or in order 'to complete the scheme of nature.' But this is . . . merely a restatement of the fact. Nor is it consistent with itself; . . . by whatever steps [vestigial organs] . . . may have been degraded into their present useless condition, [they] are the record of a former state of things, and have been retained solely through the power of inheritance . . . On the view of descent with modification [evolution] we may conclude that the existence of organs in a rudimentary, imperfect, and useless condition, or quite aborted, *far from presenting a strange difficulty, as they assuredly do on the old doctrine of creation, might even have been anticipated in accordance with the views here explained* [evolution]. [emphasis ours.] Darwin (1859:346-350)

Later Darwin modified his views, concluding that vestigial organs could result from disuse as well as from natural selection:

In order to understand the existence of rudimentary organs, we have only to suppose that former progenitor possessed the parts in question in a perfect state, and that under changed habits of life they became greatly reduced, either from simple disuse, or through the natural selection of those individuals which were least encumbered with a superfluous part, aided by the other means previously indicated. Darwin (1874:24)

It is seen here that Darwin unceremoniously embraced the now abandoned philosophy of Lamarckianism, a view which he had previously opposed with vigor.

Historical Importance of Vestigial Organs as "Proof" of Macroevolution and as a Serious "Problem" for Creationists

The appendix and other "vestigial organs" were often listed as among the "strongest evidences" to disprove creationism. Dodson and Dodson concluded that:

The appendix of man is easily understandable as a degenerating legacy from ancestors with a much coarser diet, but it is inexplicable why a useless and disease-ridden structure should have been created especially to plague (humans). Dodson and Dodson (1976:49)

In their later edition Dodson and Dodson (1985:52) still expressed essentially the same view, but admitted that the appendix may have some immunological functions as part of the lymphatic system. For further discussion of the appendix as a vestigial organ, see Moody (1953:40).

Reno (1953:126-127) found that the vestigial organ argument was used as proof of evolution in fully 73% of the high school biology textbooks that she reviewed. In 1980 Wolfrom reviewed 15 high school biology books which were up for adoption in Indiana. In seven of these the authors plainly cited the presence of vestigial organs as evidence for evolution— Wolfrom (1989). In a 1977 text on evolution with a foreword by George Gaylord Simpson, Grant noted that vestigial organs were still commonly being presented as evidence for evolution—see also Scadding (1981). In a chapter on the creation/evolution controversy, Grant cited seven supposed "proofs" of macroevolution, the sixth being vestigial organs. Relative to these organs, he remarked that vestigial organs cannot be explained by creationists:

> These structures [vestigial organs] are interpreted as reduced vestiges of their well-developed homologous in other members of the same major group. The subgroup possessing the rudimentary organ entered into a habitat or way of life in which the formerly functional organ was no longer useful, and it was greatly reduced by selection, but vestiges of it persist as phylogenetic remnants. *There is no good explanation for the existence of useless rudimentary organs in the doctrine of creationism.* [emphasis ours] Grant (1977:374)

Along the same line, Storer and Usinger concluded that vestigial organs cause problems for the special creationists, claiming that vestigial organs are useless and reduced size:

> Structures without use and of reduced size are termed vestigial organs. *From the standpoint of special creation these organs are difficult to explain; from that of evolution they are obviously features that were functional and necessary in their ancestors* but are now *in the process of disappearing from living organisms.* [emphasis ours.] Storer and Usinger (1977: 208)

Merrell claimed that:

> ... many vestigial organs have lost their adaptive function, and it may be well asked why they should continue to persist ... [and why man] ... is virtually a walking museum from his head to his feet. Merrell (1962:101)

Merrell also assumed that organs and structures which are no longer used will somehow disappear, although their final loss may take thousands of years.

Historically some researchers such as Baitsell (1929:220) have been less emphatic than the foregoing writers, calling vestigial organs only a "... valuable line of evidence" for human evolution. But others, like Parker, treated vestigial organs as if they were explicable only in terms of macroevolutionism:

> *If animals were specially created why should there be included in their bodies parts that are quite useless and often in fact positively detrimental to them?* Why . . . should man possess a system of functionless muscles for his external ear, a useless hairy covering before birth, and a worse than useless vermiform appendix? *No advocate of the theory of special creation has ever been able to give a satisfactory answer to these questions.* To those who believe in special creation *the presence of vestigial organs has proved a stumbling block that they have never been able to avoid.* In fact, the occurrence of organs of this type has always been an insuperable obstacle to the acceptance of this view of [individual creation] . . . Parker (1928:46-47) [emphasis ours.]

Parker continued this discussion by asserting that vestigial organs are exactly what would be expected in terms of evolutionism and that they are

> . . . relics whose significance can be truly understood only if they are viewed from the standpoint of the evolutionist. These relics are vestigial organs and it is in this way, and in this way only, that such organs can be understood. Parker (1928:47)

Newman likewise concluded that vestigial structures by themselves "prove" human evolutionary descent:

> It is however, of great importance to add that these [vestigial] structures are of such general occurrence throughout both the vegetable and animal kingdoms that, as Darwin has observed, it is almost impossible to find a single species which does not in this way bear some record of its own descent from other species; and the more closely the structure of any species is examined anatomically, the more numerous are such records found to be. Thus, for example, of all organisms that of man has been most minutely investigated by anatomists . . . the number of obsolescent structures which we all present in our own person is so remarkable, that their combined testimony to our descent from a quadrumanous ancestry appears to me in itself conclusive evidence [of evolution] . . . even if these structures stood alone, or apart from any more general evidences of our family relationships, they would be sufficient to *prove* our parentage. [emphasis ours] Newman (1932:74)

Throughout these quotations from evolutionary writers there is the tacit underlying assumption that if even a few organs could be shown to be useless vestiges of structures that previously functioned, this would constitute evidence disproving a design model of orgins. There is nothing in the design model, however, which would conflict with the presence of some vestigial organs. The existence of a vestigial organ would support the belief that some highly functional structure had undergone changes by which it became less functional or even useless. These data would be accommodated easily in the design model as evidence that degenerative changes have occurred since the time of creation. The presence of vestigial organs would support only de-evolution; they would not refute design.

Surveys of Vestigial Organ Discussions in Textbooks

Vestigial organs are commonly cited in textbooks as one of the strongest evidences for evolution. Webb and Vinal (1934) found in their survey of biology courses that, of those teachers who taught evolution in detail, the majority discussed vestigial structures as an important evidence of evolution. While they sometimes are still used today, vestigial organs are typically given at best, only a very brief treatment. Sweeping statements such as the following which were at one time common, are seen less frequently today:

> Among natural occurrences nothing is so difficult to understand, except from the evolutionary standpoint, as vestigial organs. These organs are really signs of the past; they afford as *indisputable a proof of the correctness of the evolutionary view as can reasonably be expected.* [emphasis ours.] Parker (1928:48).

Scadding (1981) reviewed recent college evolutionary textbooks and found that if the topic of vestigial organs was mentioned at all, no more than a few paragraphs were included. These often reflected considerable ignorance about the subject.

Skogg (1980) in a study of 93 representative secondary school biology textbooks tabulated the number of words devoted to vestigial organs in various decades—see also Skogg (1966) and Webb and Vinal (1934). From 1900 to 1977, a total of 9,641 words was devoted to the vestigial organ argument in the textbooks he selected.

A.	1900-1919	60	E. 1950-1959	878
B.	1919-1929	696	F. 1960-1969	2,378
C.	1930-1939	2,075	G. 1970-1977	973
D.	1940-1949	2,381		

There is considerable fluctuation evident here between decades. Note the decline in the 1950's despite the increase in the number of total words found in the 1960's.

While Drummond in 1903 listed over 70 supposed vestiges, Scadding (1981:173) noted that very few modern textbook authors still claim that such a large number exists. On the other hand, Storer and Usinger, in their popular textbook (1977:220) stated that "... fully 90 vestigial ... [organs] can be found in the human body." Scadding (1981) drew attention to the peculiar fact that although certain biology textbook authors still claim there are about 100 vestigial organs in the human body, they subsequently proceed to list only five or six. Scadding summarized this trend by stating that "As our knowledge has increased, the list of vestigial organs has decreased."

Is the Vestigial Organ Controversy a "Dead Horse"?

Some biologists have abandoned the vestigial organ argument, having assumed that such rejection is widespread in the scientific community. One noted origins worker, for example, recently told one of us that any further critical discussion of the whole vestigial organ issue is akin to "beating a dead horse."

Recently, some evolutionists like Loftin have abandoned certain of the vestigial organ data as supportive of macroevolution:

> Vestigial organs are one of the main lines of evidence for evolution, but much that has been said about them seems far-fetched. It has been suggested, for example, that the human vermiform appendix is a vestigial intestine. This seems to be no more plausible than the absurd idea that since human males have under developed breasts there must have been a time when both males and females nursed the young... Many male mammals have underdeveloped breasts, but nobody regards them as vestiges of a time when both sexes nursed. Loftin (1988:26).

Selected quotations from a leading evolutionist ought to dispel the notion that the classic vestigial organ argument has been totally abandoned. Awbrey (1983:6) expressed his firm belief that the teeth in fetal baleen whales and the extra mammary glands found in some females (bat, whale, and human) are completely functionless vestiges. According to Awbrey the whale teeth are "... the whales' evolutionary leftovers." He argued that such data "... clearly refute design." According to Awbrey the extra milk glands of certain female mammals fit only with the idea:

> ... that bats, whales and humans all share a common ancestor that had multiple mammae along the milk line, and was neither bat, whale nor human. Awbrey (1983:6)

Many other quotations show that vestigial organ argumentation is still popular among evolutionists. One of these authors suggested that the ability of evolution to explain vestigial organs is its crowning importance:

> Some may question why evolution should be given such special treatment. It should be because nothing else in biology explains the existence of embryonic structures (like gill slits) that are absent in adults. Nothing else adequately explains vestigial structures and homologies. Nothing else undergirds as much of ecology, taxonomy and behavior as evolution does. Without evolution, both the fact and the theory, meaningful biology is impossible. Tatina (1989:279)

Thus, the classic vestigial organ concept is alive and well in biology even though it has undergone repeated fluctuations in the amount of textbook discussion given to it.

The Vestigial Organ Concept as an Evidence Against the Belief in Design

The vestigial organ argument has been used from Darwin's time forward, primarily to discredit creationism. Scadding discovered this criticism of creationism in Haeckel's discussions of vestigial organs:

> Haeckel makes clear why this line of argument [concerning vestigial organs] was of such importance to early evolutionary biologists. Nineteenth century creationists had held to the position that the creation of man and the animals by God was 'perfect' and hence the observations of organs which had no apparent function proved something of an embarrassment to them. Functionless organs were clearly a distinct embarrassment to anyone who wished to talk of the purpose of nature. Haeckel refers to these rudimentary organs as a dysteleological proof of evolution. . . . Scadding (1983:5)

Although most evolutionary scientists use vestigial organs as an evidence against only the strict creationist views, Rensch even tried to use them to refute "theistic evolutionists" who profess that God merely directed evolution.

> . . . [vestigial organs] render comprehensible the existence of biologically tolerable faults of construction in nature, which would not have come to exist if evolution were directed [theistic evolution]. Rensch (1959:67-68)

To further support his argument for a totally non-directed evolution, Rensch added:

> We need only to recall the incomplete system of blood circulation in *Amphibia*, the vagina duplex of *Marsupialia*, the growth followed by nutritive reabsorption of embryos at a certain stage of the development in *Salamandra atra*, the formation of atypical infertile spermatozoa in *Bithynia*, the useless development of the genitalia in bee workers and the numerous cases of vestigial organs (such as nonfunctioning limb rudiments of *Python*, *Seps* and *Balaena*). Rensch (1959: 67-68)

Rensch and others have tried to show that vestigial organs would not even occur by evolution, if the evolution were directed, in effect asserting that a Designer would not have used theistic evolution under any circumstances. As shown earlier, this argument that vestigial organs refute all design is false because the loss of designed functions in certain organs is easily accommodated in the design model as degeneration, not evolution.

Dysteleology—An Evolutionary Theology

The vestigial organ argument is thus part of a broader attack that Haeckel, Rensch, and some contemporary macroevolutionists like Dawkins (1986) have leveled at the design model; they have asserted that there is bad design in biology, a criticism that is called dysteleology. The argument of bad design has been used by Awbrey against creationist claims that the disappearing teeth in developing whales may have a function:

> Fetal baleen whales develop a full set of teeth, many with the tricuspid form characteristic of their land-dwelling ancestors. These teeth never erupt through the gums and are resorbed completely before birth. This fact agrees with other evidence from fossils and comparative anatomy. All fit descent with modification beautifully. These teeth are the whale's evolutionary leftovers.... Unlike the evolutionary alternative, it [creationism] has no independent support. *It also is counter-intuitive because it asks us to believe that a creator who could blink an entire universe into existence couldn't design a toothless whale to develop without teeth.* Biology contains myriad examples that demolish such *ad hoc* ideas. [emphasis ours.] Awbrey (1983:6)

Awbrey thus asserted that to avow creationism in the face of these tooth data would demand attributing low intelligence, lack of skill, or clumsy planning to the Creator. As Scadding (1981) has noted, however, this argument from dysteleology is not a *scientific* support for macro-evolutionism but is instead a theological discussion of the Creator's attributes—what some people believe God would or would not do. Thus Loftin was discussing theology, not science, when he asserted that:

> If the creator created blind cave animals especially for subterranean environments, there does not seem to be any convincing reason why he would have given them eyes at all, of *any* kind or at *any* stage of their life cycle. Loftin (1988:25).

Awbrey spoke theologically, not scientifically, when he implied that no creator would design a whale's jaw to have teeth which are absorbed before birth. Dysteleology has thus become a popular theology among certain evolutionists, not because it is based on scientific logic favoring evolutionism but because it seems to be a useful argument against creationism. In a later section we shall examine whale teeth, the human pharynx, and other supposed instances of dysteleology.

Does the Vestigial Organ Argument Stifle Research?

Byers (1983:2) argued that evolutionary vestigial organ logic is actually a form of "anti-knowledge"; the evolutionary worker researches an organ like the appendix with the preconceived belief that it "must have no function." Such a negative mindset becomes a stumbling block in the pathway of discovering an organ's actual functions. Perhaps much delay in deducing the functions of these organs has already resulted from the macroevolutionary belief that they are vestigial and hence "ought to be" functionless.

Scadding (1981) identified another logical problem with the vestigial organ argument: to assert that any organ is vestigial is an attempt to prove that a function for that organ does not exist. However, science can deal only with what can be observed; science has nothing to say about the non-existence of functions or the non-existence of anything. Hence the vestigial organ argument is not a scientific discussion. The most one could conclude from science would be that no functions have yet been observed for a particular organ. To say that none exist would go far outside the domain of science.

Four Types of So-Called Vestigial Organs

Scadding (1981) divided Wiedersheim's vestigial organ list into four general groups or types. The first group includes vestigial organs which have been incorrectly identified because they serve biological functions. Examples of this group include the pineal, pituitary, and lachrymal glands.

Wiedersheim's second group, which contains the majority of the list, includes small non-secreting structures that have function, but because of their very small size have only limited or minor roles. Examples include the wisdom teeth, the phalanges of the third, fourth, and fifth toes, and the valves of certain veins.

In the third group are structures that function only or primarily during some stage of development. Examples of this group are the notochord, the posterior cardinal veins, and the ducts of Cuvier. Structures which function only during part of the organism's life, or as a back-up only under certain circumstances, are not vestigial in the classical sense; they clearly serve a purpose, even if only during emergencies or in certain developmental stages.

Within Wiedersheim's fourth category are those organs which are developmental "remnants" of the reproductive structures of the opposite sex such as male nipples, the male Mullerian ducts, and the female Wolffian duct, all of which occur in human embryonic development. Scadding, however, stressed that organs in this fourth group of Wiedersheim's do not demonstrate macroevolutionary descent:

> These structures, however, clearly reflect the embryonic development of a sexually dimorphic organism which begins its development in a sexually indifferent condition with structures characteristic of both sexes. They certainly do not reflect phylogenetic development. No one supposes males evolved from females or vice versa. Scadding (1983:5)

Functions Found for "Useless" Organs

As the knowledge of physiology increased, it was found that most, if not all, of these organs which were thought to be vestigial clearly have in important function (some a vital function) in the body. Scadding (1981:174) concluded that Wiedersheim was wrong; most of those organs listed as vestigial do play some role.

Prime examples of organs which were at one time labeled vestigial include even the pituitary, adrenal, and lachrymal glands as well as the pancreas and the spleen. Today, fewer than six structures are regarded by anyone as vestigial in humans, and a large body of evidence exists supporting the position that even these are not actually vestigial. Ahead of his time, Goodrich concluded many years ago that every organ has a function:

> Every day naturalists are discovering the functions of the most insignificant-looking organs. Little importance can be attached to the statement often made that the characters which distinguish nearly allied species are of no value to them; in fact no . . . [structure or organ] should be accepted as useless until it has been definitely proved that it exerts no influence on the death-rate. Some few years ago . . . it was held [that] such organs . . . as the thyroid gland, the pituitary gland, the suprarenal glands, and others, are useless structures, functionless vestigial remnants. They are now known to be of the greatest importance, altering the composition of the blood or secreting substances essential for the regulation of . . . metabolism. He would be a rash man indeed who would now assert that any part of the human body is useless. Goodrich (1924:124-125)

The fact that researchers are increasingly finding one or more uses for organs that were formerly labeled vestigial suggests that a use for other claimed vestigial organs may someday be found as well. Yablokov (1974: Chap. 6) discussed at length the difficulty of identifying vestigial organs by analyzing in detail the alleged vestigial organs of marine mammals. Scadding (1981:175) concluded that ". . . in practice it is difficult if not impossible to unambiguously identify organs totally lacking in function."

The function of many organs thought to be vestigial may be crucial during certain stages of development, but less crucial in other stages. Well-known examples of this include the appendix, the thyroid, and the pineal gland. Birdsell gave the following excellent example of the foregoing principle, showing that the notochord fulfills its destiny early in the human embryonic development:

> . . . all mammals, including ourselves, in their embryological stages, retain a *notochord,* a cartilaginous rod which was present in the early ancestors of the true vertebrates, those with segmented backbones. It might seem ridiclous to retain this outmoded structure in such highly organized creatures as the mammals. But if we look at development as a process, it becomes clear that the cells which form the notochord are very closely connected with organizing and bringing into being the essential structure which forms the long axis of the fetus. That is, the spinal cord, the brain, the heart, kidneys, and segments of muscle are all involved. Since the notochord provides this organizing function, its cells must be retained in the early fetal stage of mammalian development. The explanation

of many so-called vestigial organs probably lies in the role they play in furthering the organization of other structures in the growth of the embryo. Birdsell (1972:52)

It Would Be Difficult to Prove That an Organ is Functionless

An organ never could be proved scientifically to be functionless—see Zimmerman (1959:116-117) and also Scadding (1981:173-176). Even if a structure were surgically removed and no discernible effect on the patient could be determined, it still could not be assumed tht the organ was functionless. Perhaps other organs assumed its functions and hence its removal caused no major noticeable problems.

As Reno (1953:47) has noted, the importance of body organs differs. The loss of vital organs like the heart or brain causes immediate death; the removal of many organs that are less essential, however, like the spleen or stomach, may not affect the organism for some time, if at all—see Guyton (1966). All organs, including the vital organs, could be ranked according to their importance. Parker (1928:35) stressed that before we can label an organ vestigial, it must ". . . not only [be removed] without detriment . . . but must actually be shown to be without function." Whenever any particular vestigial organ is shown to have a function, then macroevolution is no longer the only possible explanation of its origin. In this book we attempt to show that most, if not all, supposedly vestigial organs clearly have necessary functions; they fit with a designed creation rather than a chance-based evolutionary origin.

**If A Structure Were Really Useless,
Would It Be Expected to Disappear?**

Several hypotheses are used by evolutionists to explain the slow loss of what they label "vestigial" organs. According to the most common hypothesis, these organs were at one time functional, but "lost" much of their usefulness in the course of evolutionary history and thus are slowly degenerating. But, there is no biological mechanism to ensure that loss of use would in itself cause the loss of the organ.

In the Lamarckian model, organs are said to deteriorate through successive generations solely because they are "not used." Lamarckism has been shown to be without merit and thus unacceptable to most biologists today. Steele's (1981) controversial and now disregarded work with mice has been the only well known attempt in recent years to support Lamarckism—see Zimmerman (1959:116). Yet, it is often believed by the public, and tacitly assumed even in scientific circles, that an organ which is not used will somehow eventually disappear on its own. The experimental evidence is unequivocal that if an organ is not used, it will be underdeveloped, but disuse alone will not cause it to undergo a total loss in future generations.

Macroevolutionists now teach that in order for a body part to disappear in the future, nature must actively select against it, meaning that the structure must be directly deleterious to survival. If, for example, an appendage is not used and yet does not adversely affect survival, macroevolutionists should expect it to remain for eons, perhaps until the animal itself becomes extinct. For an appendage to disappear, that organ must make the organism as a whole less fit to survive, thereby causing the organism to lose out in the competition for survival or reproduction. Many macroevolutionists thus believe that for an organ to be totally lost, it must impede locomotion, health, or body functioning *before* the stage in which the organism gives birth to its last offspring. There is no mechanism that would cause an organ totally to disappear simply because it is no longer useful.

Does Evolutionism Lead to Self-Contradictory Predictions Regarding Vestigial Organs?

If the foregoing evolutionary logic were correct, we would expect a large number of vestigial organs to exist because no demonstrated mechanism exists for the total elimination of organs that have become merely useless. Most vestigial organs, especially smaller ones, would not affect survival adversely; their mere presence would not threaten the species. Because macroevolutionists would not expect vestigial organs to be completely eradicated by evolution, the demonstrated lack of vestiges is strong evidence against macroevolution.

But evolutionary logic is flexible, so that one might argue the exact opposite: that no organ would ever have been expected to lose its functions or to become vestigial in the first place. Consider evolutionary logic as it applies to an organ that has only a minor function; the existing function of that organ would nevertheless be preserved and enhanced, as Scadding noted that:

> . . . natural selection would be expected to operate even if a structure has only a minor adaptive advantage . . . Fisher . . . has shown that only when the selection coefficient is less than the reciprocal of the population size would natural selection cease to be effective. Prout (1964) goes further and states that evolutionary theory in general would be in trouble if the efficacy of very mild selection were in doubt. Scadding (1983:5)

The whole basis of Darwinian evolution is selection of minor variations that confer very small advantages. If *any* function at all existed for an organ, in the macroevolutionist's view that organ would be expected to develop gradually into a more useful structure instead of becoming vestigial.

Using macroevolutionism, two self contradictory predictions have thus emerged: (1) there should be no vestigial organs because any existing functions would never be lost but improved; (2) there should be numerous vestigial organs because once organs become completely useless, they would never be removed by natural selection.

According to the first of these conflicting predictions, macroevolution would never have been expected to produce vestigial organs. In that light, macroevolutionists like Darwin and Wiedersheim were at odds with their own origins model when they originally proposed the vestigial organ argument years ago.

Do Vestigial Organs "Prove Too Much?"

Another problem with the vestigial organ view is that many organs which are labeled vestigial in the human body "... prove too much," to use the words of Klotz (1970:135). Klotz used as an example the so-called "vestigial" mammary glands in the male which "... might suggest that at one time males suckled the young," an idea that no macroevolutionists have as yet propounded, as far as we know. Mammary glands will be discussed in greater detail in Section II.

Also, Reno (1970:81, 86) asserted that if we assume that one particular birth abnormality (such as humans born with tails) has phylogentic significance, we must take all birth abnormalities into account. If the appearance of a human caudal appendage suggests that we descended from tail-bearing forebears, perhaps the harelip condition should be taken to mean that we are likewise closely allied to the rabbits. Instead, consistency requires the conclusion that all birth defects are merely abnormalities and that none of them alone can be used to demonstrate phylogenetic ancestry.

Chiu (1983:1) reasoned that the presence of extra fingers or toes does not prove that man's ancestors had more than five digits on each limb. By the same token he asserted that biologists ought to also refrain from using other mutation-based abnormalities (such as whale leg bones or extra mammary glands) to deduce ancestries. Bergman (1990).

Vestigial Organ Discussions in The Popular Media—Lamarckian Philosophy Still Runs Rampant

Authors of articles in popular media sometimes imply that changes in vestigial organs are a result of disuse alone. In the Compton's Picture Encyclopedia for example, the author stated the penguin's wings changed into flippers when these birds ceased to fly and began to swim:

> Ages ago the penguin could fly as well as any other seabird. Now its wings are short, paddle-like flappers, entirely useless for flight. The bird has lived for ages in or near the arctic regions, where it has few human or animal enemies. Thus, it came to spend all its time on land or in the water. For generations, it did not fly. In the course of long evolution, its wings became small and stiff and lost their long feathers. Now they cannot be moved in the middle joint like the wings of flying birds [can]. Compton's Picture Encyclopedia (1956: 162)

It is usually assumed by evolutionists that the penguin's remote ancestors could fly quite well, but as their environment changed they no longer "needed" to fly to survive. Logically it would seem that any mutations which reduced efficient wing use would have also impeded survival and would thus have been selected against. Any that aided swimming would be positively selected for. This would theoretically result in the improvement of *both* skills, not the loss of one.

All such explanations are actually lapses into Lamarckism. The encyclopedia author actually used the Larmarckian theory of acquired characteristics, attributing purposive thought to penguin evolution:

> The penguin . . . became a good swimmer and diver. They use their wings as a swimmer uses his arms in a crawl stroke. They steer with their feet. Compton's Picture Encyclopedia (1956:162).

Obviously, the paddle-like flippers do not function as wings. They do function quite well to enable the penguin to swim and thus are not vestigial; nor is there evidence (fossil or otherwise) that penguins previously were able to fly. If one is to call the swimming wings of penguins vestigial, then by the same faulty reasoning, human arms could be called vestigial front legs. Darwin was not sure if the penguins' wings were vestigial or nascent, but he believed that they were either one or the other (Darwin 1859:346)—also see Hedtke (1983:127-128). Again we note that, based on evolution, it is difficult to conclude whether an organ is "coming or going."

In a humorous parody of modern living, Gaines (1964:94) commented on the increased use of motor vehicles for locomotion instead of walking such that

> . . . in time, our legs will become vestigial organs, and will end up soft and flat, looking like round bottom toy dolls.

Even in biological and scientific works, statements such as ". . . this organ is gradually disappearing because it is not used any more," are common. Goodrich assumed that unused body organs will somehow degenerate:

> Unless [vestigial organs] vary in such a way as to become adapted to fulfill some new function—they are apt to disappear. Degeneration, in fact, is a widespread phenomenon among animals and plants, and leads to the loss of any special structures, mental or bodily, which the organism no longer needs in the particular environment for which it has become adapted. Goodrich (1924: 139-140)

As noted previously, Darwin himself (1859:349) embraced the erroneous disuse concept as he wrote: ". . . it appears probable that disuse has been the main agent in rendering organs rudimentary [vestigial]." There is a widespread belief that disuse alone can cause the loss of an organ, even though the concept is counter to most interpretations of macroevolutionism as well as most of the existing empirical evidence. The disuse argument is only one example of the widespread ignorance regarding the subject of vestigial structures, both on the part of the reading public and professional biologists.

The Loss Mutation View of Vestigial Organ Origin

Instead of the disuse view, some evolutionists have suggested that useless organs gradually disappear through "loss mutations." But this phraseology simply labels rather than explains what happens. Believers in the concept of loss mutations postulate that certain recurrent gene mutations can cause the loss of an organ or even an entire organ system.

Natural selection would not be expected to favor loss mutations for a useless structure unless its loss would also cause a reduction in the incidence of some types of disease or enable the body to use its resources better. If an organ did not have survival value it would seem that the organisms involved would continue to exist at the same level whether or not the organ were present. Genes for such useless structures would be expected to remain at about the same percentage in the gene pools. The percentage of the genes coding for useless organs would change only if the mutation producing or causing the loss of an organ would somehow also cause a clear survival advantage. Even if such loss mutations for organs exist, they are extremely rare. At best, they would merely create more variability in the total gene pool, and would not totally eliminate any genotype because there appears to be no mechanism by which the loss mutation for a very minor organ would infiltrate any gene pool to a high percentage.

According to macroevolutionists, total elimination of an organ would require that the organ become detrimental to survival and reproduciton. There would be little selection expected for or against genes controlling most vestigial organs since they would have very low selection coefficients—see Howe and Davis (1971). Whether the animals had the vestigial organ or not would depend mostly upon chance; hence, the loss mutation concept fails to explain vestigiality.

A single "loss mutation" would likely cause the disappearance of only one aspect of an organ because most organs such as the tonsils, ear muscles, and *os coccyx* are under the control of many genes. The same loss mutation would probably also affect some other body structures adversely. The genetic control of any one organ in humans is highly interrelated to other organs. Change in the genes governing one organ often causes adverse alterations in other unrelated organs.

If a gene has mutated, the DNA of that locus is still present and undergoes "back-mutation" at a given rate. Unless all the loci governing a vestigial organ were actually removed from the genome, as by chromosomal aberrations, the loss mutations could experience back-mutation. This would mean that the potential for the restoration of that theoretically functionless organ would remain a permanent part of "the gene pool."

Efforts to accelerate evolution through bombardment of fruit flies (*Drosophila*) and other short-lived animals with ionizing radiation have not produced direct evidence for mutations that would cause permanent and total loss of body structures. The idea of loss mutations is thus insufficient to account for organs becoming vestigial and finally disappearing.

Do Homeotic Mutations Help Explain The Origin of New Organs?

There are examples in the genetics of *Drosophila* of "homeotic" mutations in which a certain organ of the fly such as a wing can be changed into an entirely different structure such as a haltere or balancer. Ouweneel (1975) has reviewed and expanded the study of homeotic mutants in *Drosophila* showing that the eye area can produce wing-like outgrowths or the antennae can form legs. He concluded that homeotic mutations are no benefit in evolution but simply produce bizarre modifications of existing organs. They do not produce "new organs" nor do they lead to the loss or elimination of existing organs. They merely cause existing organ types to occur at other locations on the insect.

Negative Allometry and Vestigial Organs

In another hypothetical mechanism called "negative allometry," certain evolutionists have proposed that organs which are vestigial will eventually disappear because biological building materials are limited. The highly functional organs will utilize these limited supplies first, to the detriment of structures that are less functional or even vestigial.

An example involves lizards whose limbs become relatively shorter with increasing body size. About these shrunken lizard legs, Rensch (1959:223) concluded that "As no special selection was at work to preserve the legs, they become more and more reduced." He implied here that special selection is required to preserve organs, or they will automatically become reduced and ultimately will disappear on their own.

Rensch's idea of negative allometry has little support in the literature, and his supposed examples of it can be explained more adequately in keeping with a design model. One who holds to negative allometry ascribes some type of vitalistic "thrift" or "purpose" to the organism, enabling it to conserve its resources ever more effectively. Outside of the Designer's activity, however, there is little basis for such design teleology. Further discussion of negative allometry occurs in section II as a possible explanation for adult blindness in cave-dwelling creatures.

Panmixia and Reversal of Selection as Explanations for Vanishing Vestigial Organs

Lull (1932) accounted for the disappearance of vestigial organs according to two principles: (1) "panmixia" and (2) "selection reversal." In the panmixia principle the organ would no longer be useful as a result of a change in the creature's environment or habitat. Accordingly, natural selection would cease to retain the organ. In Lull's panmixia view, if natural selection did not act in a positive way to preserve the organ, the organ would disappear of its own accord.

Similar words "panmixia" or "panmixis" have come into widespread usage in population genetics to designate a situation in which there is no selection for or against the various alleles of a given locus. This concept has become synonymous with random mating—see Hartl (1980:132) and Jacquard (1970:47-48). Lack of selection for or against the genes that produce a certain organ would produce a state of panmixis, but this by itself would not lead to the loss of the organ unless somehow the organ's presence became detrimental.

In Lull's "selection reversal" view, a useless organ is a physical or nutritional burden on the animal, and thus, its absence increases an organism's chances of reproduction. The organ consequently undergoes a "negative selection." While it is thereby in the process of being selected out of an animal line, the organ would be considered "vestigial" as long as it is still present. This seems to be the most viable evolutionary explanation for loss of organs and may apply to the genesis of blind cave creatures. Even so, the selection reversal process appears to be feasible only if the organ is large and definitely detrimental; these conditions seldom would be met.

The "Law" of Material Compensation and Vestigial Organs

The so-called "Law" of material compensation is a phenomenon, noted by Geoffroy St. Hilaire and others, in which organs that are active during a creature's development will consume more than their share of body building material. As a result, other parts will become proportionally reduced in size.

Eimer (1901) claimed, for example, that during development of mammals, the formation of stronger hind legs caused a reduction or even disappearance of the lumbar ribs and frequently the tail. It is assumed in the compensation view that only a limited quantity of nutrients exists in the body. Those structures that are growing faster or utilizing more energy will have a stronger drawing power, thereby nutritionally depriving the parts that are growing less rapidly and slowing their growth substantially.

According to Rensch (1959:180) the principle of material compensation has been neglected in recent years. Rensch's concept of "negative allometry," discussed earlier, is virtually the same as the "law of material compensation." Both ideas, in turn, are similar to the old Lamarckian idea of disuse and they experience the same difficulties. In his *Origin of Speices,* Darwin noted that what seemed like evidence for body compensation may have resulted instead from natural selection eliminating all animal variants which have superfluous body material.

One way to study the extent and limits of the compensatory process in animals is to perform experiments involving anatomical alterations during development. In young rabbits and guinea pigs, for example, the extirpation of a testicle or an ovary results in hypertrophy (increased growth) of the remaining gonad—Pasewaldt (1888), and Hackenbruch (1888). Ribbert (1894) removed five out of eight mammary buds in two month old rabbits. The remaining mammary glands manifested clear hypertrophy. In adult salamanders, Kochs (1897) found hypertrophy of both the hind legs and the tail after the front legs had been amputated.

The above cases illustrate what is called "functional load hypertrophy." Many examples of "material compensation" may have more to do with the response of the organism to physically traumatic situations and problems caused by mutilation than they have to do with compensation. If several of the mammary buds in rabbits are removed, for example, it follows that the remaining glands become more active. Removing a body part enables the remaining parts to absorb and use more nutrients which are now more available, given the same food intake.

Although neighboring organs can be reduced in any individual animal by the process of material compensation, no evidence exists that the effects of such changes are inherited, causing alteration of the structure in future generations. The only way the change would be heritable is if both the original change was genetic, and the resultant compensatory alterations caused a greater likelihood of survival during the reproductive years.

The theory of compensation, however, may still be a valid non-evolutionary explanation in both man and animals for the atrophy of some organs which appear to be vestigial. Perhaps it applies to development under particular restricted situations, such as with reduced food intake.

Rensch, who championed the material compensation concept, however, communicated caution in attributing vestigial organ origin to the material compenstation mechanism when he wrote that:

> ... only a few examples have been sufficiently analyzed as yet, and ... it is very difficult to prove that a certain result is due to material compensation, especially in those cases where the material consumed by strongly growing parts is not taken from the adjacent organs. Rensch (1959:187)

Despite these cautious admissions, Rensch still placed great faith in material compensation as a means of reducing organs:

> Compensatory phenomena seem to have an especially important bearing on the process of phyletic reductions of organs, as in most cases these cannot be explained by selection. Rensch (1959:187)

It can be concluded that the term "material compensation" merely designates a redistribution that occurs in given experiments without providing a genetic mechanism or an origins explanation for vestigial organs.

Some of the So-Called Vestigial Organs May Result from a Developmental Plan

Wilder-Smith (1968:106) proposed another explanation for the existence of vestigial organs; the similarity of the biochemistry of all living forms stems from a common basic developmental plan. For this reason one would expect to find similar physiological, biochemical and anatomical structures in all living organisms—especially in animals of the same family. Macroevolutionists assume this developmental similarity has resulted from necessity, whereas anti-evolutionists like Wilder-Smith see it as evidence of activity by a common Designer.

Wilder-Smith concluded that in *Homo sapiens* there is a "physiological necessity" that an embryo be capable of becoming either male or female:

> Obviously man and other mammals must have the chance of becoming either male or female [which is determined at conception] during their development, so that the basis of both sexes must be present in all organisms . . . On this basis the presence of both types of sex organs in either sex becomes a physiological necessity, so that by change in hormone function and concentration the male or female structure may be developed at will. Wilder-Smith (1968:109)

In the design origins model it is concluded that traits like mammae and nipples appearing on males are a necessary part of the total intelligent developmental plan. Similarly, a certain embryological structure in the rabbit may develop into a digestive organ while in another species, like man, it becomes smaller, as in the case of the appendix, and serves a secretory function.

A similar situation occurs in automobile design. One basic automobile, usually the sedan, is first developed; then it is modified to produce hard tops, station wagons, convertibles, and other models. Economy requires as little deviation from the basic plan as possible in the origin of the non-standard models. With living creatures, economy also requires a basic design on which there are no more modifications than are necessary to produce the great variety of life. This view, which dates back to Linnaeus' idea of "archetypes," is just now being explored and its full understanding will require a greater knowledge of embryology, biochemistry, and genetics than presently exists. Denton (1986) noted that especially in the field of taxonomy, biologists are returning to pre-Darwinian and non-evolutionary ideologies. It is a fascinating area, ripe for further scientific exploration.

Coding Theory and Organs Falsely Labeled "Vestigial"

Pittman (1983:3) has proposed a mechanism to account for the presence of certain supposed vestigial organs as well as some birth abnormalities such as extra nipples, extra fingers, the so-called "caudal appendage" on certain babies, and the abnormal leg bones in some whales. He suggested that the Designer coded for the number and position of bones in all vertebrate animals by means of one basic DNA code package. The Designer then superimposed additional codes on these "tightly coded packages" by overriding certain aspects of the main code to achieve individual differences and even to produce what we call "vestigial organs." In the whale, for example, a special override code pattern would modify hip bones and limb bones generally present in mammals.

Pittman further theorized that errors could sometimes creep through, as in the case where individual Cetaceans may actually produce leg bones, or human females may have extra nipples. Pittman originally described this coding model as follows:

> ... the information for the construction of all living organisms, be they flies or whales or people, complete with all so-called vestigial organs (wings, legs, etc.), is encoded in the DNA chains for the respective organisms' gene pool. Curiously, this is a binary code just like the computers we all know and love ... With such a binary code we can (in principle) count the number of bits that fully define a whale or a fly ... For larger organisms it is a stupendously large number of bits, which is the whole point. The more bits there, the greater chance of error.
>
> Coding theory would predict that a wise and purposeful Designer would eliminate bit patterns that cannot occur in viable creatures by encoding the bits more compactly, thus reducing the total number of bits.
>
> Consider, for example, the bone structure of vertebrates. The number of bits required to encode all possible numbers of bones of all possible shapes in all possible relative positions is astronomical. But we do not see any such variety in real organisms, living or fossil. Instead there is exactly one backbone, with the head bones connected to it at one end. Limbs come in pairs, usually two near the head and two at the other end, but never more than two pair (except in monsters). And so on.
>
> The evolutionist speculates that the skeletal system is a gradual accumulation of the genetic codes specifying the various components of it, with the more viable bit patterns surviving and the less viable dying out. Because the pattern we observe has great survival value, none of the other possibilities have survived, but subsequent evolution; has only modified the basic patterns in small ways. Pittman (1983:3ff)

Pittman reasoned that such a design alternative is superior to the atavistic organ view of evolution. He maintained that tests could be performed to show which view best fits the data:

> This then is the prediction from design: when the genetic codes are unraveled for the larger organisms, the creationist would expect to see tightly-coded packages of genetic codes which are responsible for entire structures in the organism. There will be no rational or obvious relationship between the components of the code and the components of the structure defined by it: skeletons will not be defined by the aggregate of the codes for the individual bones.

The prediction of descent with modification, as Awbrey calls his version of evolution, would be to find primitive genetic patterns with perhaps a few bits modified, and various random accumulations of codes, each of which defines one specific component of the resulting organism, or is perhaps kept on as "baggage" and suppressed by other specific patterns.

The difference between these two predictions should be clear. Both "explain" the so-called vestigial organs, and the explanations are similar. But the differences are testable, and should be as apparent to the trained observer as the difference between a well-designed, optimized, program and a hodgepodge of sundry subroutines loosely stuck together by a bunch of incompetent hackers. Pittman (1983:3ff)

Recently Pittman (1989) has expanded his discussion of coding theory as it relates to the design model or origins. He asserted that the Designer perhaps modified incidental aspects of the design in one species without discarding the whole critical core of code.

Pittman (1989) mentioned a recent development in paradigms called "Object-Oriented Programming" (or OOP) as defined by the programming language "Small Talk." OOP has become very popular and is slated for use in future software. It is a significant change in programming methodology and ought to have lasting effects.

The unique feature of OOP is its "reusable code" and the focus is on the data objects themselves rather than the program code. Each object on an OOP environment is defined in terms of the data that characterize the object.

A key feature of OOP is that a new class of objects can be defined in terms of some other class of objects by the "reusable code." One needs specify only how the new object *differs* from the others. The new object is thus said to "inherit" all the reusable features of the parent class. New methods added to particularize the new class simply "override" the properties of the parent class that need to be changed; the rest of the code is otherwise unchanged.

In the code for a class of vehicles for transportation of people and things, for example, some of the descriptive fields for one object in the class might be "methods" concerning its length, width, load capacity, and such. One general "method" might specify how to steer the object with something like a steering wheel. Subclasses of vehicles could reflect the type of surface on which the vehicle travels such as air, land, and water. Further fields would be defined such as the number and placement of wheels as well as methods for support, locomotion, and stopping. The steering method of a particular class would by design be "overridden" in each subclass by the method needed to connect the steering wheel to the steering mechanism in that particular class of vehicle.

In Pittman's illustration (1989), terrestrial surface vehicles could have subclasses that differentiate trains, for example from passenger automobiles. A train car might have a particular "method" that overrides the steering method for other terrestrial surface vehicles, reflecting the fact that steering trains does not require a steering wheel and associated linkage. But it would "inherit" many other methods so that much of the code would in that sense be "reusable."

Pittman (1989) has applied these aspects of OOP to supposed vestigial organs. If the steering mechanism in a train is overridden, the steering wheel itself would be something like a vestigial organ in a living system. But the otherwise unused data field for the steering wheel could be adapted to effect some part of the stopping function—perhaps being used as a wheel to turn the brakes. The Designer may have used procedures similar to those found in OOP programming so that each item in a class (*e.g.* "mammal") would "inherit" a basic code, aspects of which could be overridden to produce the many different mammal variations.

Concerning Pittman's proposal of tightly coded packages with specific override packages, Crapo (1984:1ff) agreed and simply argued that all coded packages were originated and favored by natural selection. To this Pittman replied that the initial synthesis of the tightly coded packages by macroevolution would be very unlikely and would require:

> ... such a vast expenditure of effort and skill that natural selection will surely prefer any of the many possible loose and inefficient equivalents, simply because they are viable at a much earlier stage of their development. Pittman (1984:1ff)

The challenge still remains for macroevolutionists to show that tightly coded packages could have arisen gradually by natural selection—see Denton (1986).

Were All Code Packages Designed at One Time?

Pittman did not discuss the possibility that some of the override code packages may have been incorporated by the Designer into various genotypes long after the original creation. In two papers—Lammerts and Howe (1974:227) and Howe and Lammerts (1980:6)—Lammerts developed the idea that the Designer has periodically brought about rapid genetic change in the bodies of certain creatures, adapting them to specific environmental circumstances. Accordingly, Lammerts suggested that some amazing providential changes resulted in gene systems, long after the original creation had occurred. Given the basic asssumptions of a design model, Lammerts' concept is at least feasible. Although it is not accepted by all design theorists at this time, it has been adopted by some. We shall discuss this Lammerts' view as a possible explanation for the origin and geographical distribution of blind cave creatures in section II.

The Decay Principle and Some Putative Vestigial Organs

Howitt (1972) concluded that many organs which today have been labeled "vestigial" are actually the result of improper nutrition and arrested or abortive development. Habits of culture, diet, and cleanliness can contribute to phenotypic reduction in size and functional capacity of some organs. If some useless and hence "vestigial" organs did arise by genetic changes, this would be primarily evidence of decay or loss and not evolutionary development of organs into more complex or more useful structures. For a discussion of the degeneration principle and the second law of thermodynamics as they apply to origins, see Williams (1981) and H. Morris (1974:75).

Reno invoked this decay principle as a possible cause for some of the so-called vestigial organs:

> . . . let us consider how some of these organs, which have an obscure and minor use, might have degenerated from a more perfect condition. We know that God created things perfect, for when they were finished He saw that they were good. Since sin entered the world it has caused many changes, and they have usually been toward degeneration and not improvement. Before sin had time to greatly affect the human body, man lived to be hundreds of years old. Gradually his life was shortened. This may have been due to the degenerating influence of sin. It is very possible that some of our organs now may have very different degrees of usefulness from those of Adam, Enoch, and Noah. We do not know that the appendix, lymph nodes, tonsils, etc., now have the same function as they did in early Bible times. Certainly there is some reason for a shortened life span. Reno (1953:50-51)

The Concept of Overdesign

Many human organs exist either in pairs or bilaterally. Although two organs are best for depth and stereophonic perception, in many cases, only one organ or one side is actually necessary for survival. Humans can survive with one good ear, eye, lung, or kidney, for example, although these conditions may cause the affected individual to suffer some impairments or limitations of lifestyle. The fact that one can live adequately with one lung is a condition not predicted by "survival of the fittest" in a macroevolution model based on mutation and natural selection.

Macroevolutionists might argue it is not merely the ability to *live* or to *survive* but to *compete*. Yet it is not clear how such a general need to *compete* would have yielded paired organs with regularity. Overdesign in the case of paired organs can be explained more satisfactorily by the idea that a Designer built excess capacity into various organs as a protection against the vicissitudes of life. Some who object to the design model explain organ oversufficiencies as merely the result of the fact that embryos develop on a bilateral plan. Yet this bilateral plan is itself inexplicable in the macroevolution view. Both bilateral organs and those labeled vestigial find better fit with the theory of "overdesign."

Here are several examples of overdesign in the human body:
1. the number of brain cells by far exceeds the number which one would possibly need to grow to adulthood and reproduce;
2. human lung capacity exceeds the amount of air we normally inhale (the tidal capacity) or that we need (the residual capacity);
3. kidney capacity in a healthy human far exceeds the body's functional requirements;
4. the human body can support far more weight than is most often needed, and in many animals this difference is often greater than in man. The tendon in the foot of a chicken, for example, can support a weight of several hundred pounds;
5. the range of sensory reception is typically far broader than most people need for survival and reproduction.

A margin of safety is present in most body organs. The fact that humans can usually survive quite well with only one of the paired structures such as lungs, kidneys, arms, ears is also empirical evidence of "overdesign" in origins. Many organs can be removed surgically and another organ will take over some of the functions of the one that was lost.

Some organs, such as the appendix and tonsils, can be removed without any short term discernible effect on the person. Because this is true it does not follow that the supposed vestigial organ lacks a function. Anything that aids convenience, ease, life enjoyment, and effectiveness is functional and fits with the creationist idea that a provident Designer produced the many different kinds of organisms separately from each other.

Another example of overdesign is in the spleen which was once regarded as a useless vestige by many macroevolutionists. Among its numerous functions the spleen is now known to produce various types of blood cells before birth and for a short time thereafter. Because it ordinarily does not fulfill these blood forming functions in the adult, the spleen was seen by some evolutionists as vestigial, at least as far as red corpuscle production is concerned—see King and Showers (1964:303). Recently it has been found, however, that in cases of severe hemorrhage the spleen actually resumes the function of corpuscle synthesis until the emergency has passed.

The spleen is known to serve several other important functions as well, although most adults can survive without it. In case of malaria, for example, an enlarged spleen is one of the common symptoms. For some reasons that are not yet understood, a spleenectomy drastically shortens the lifespan of a small number of patients. Some evidence indicates that in these particular patients the spleen has a function that cannot be assumed by another organ after the spleen is removed.

Some macroevolutionists rationalize these data by arguing that a body which has more "spare parts" is more "fit." Selection for or against organs, though, does *not* operate past child bearing age. However, it is in the advanced adult years after reproduction that the feature of having other "spare parts" becomes more and more important. Neo-Darwinian macroevolutionary mechanisms can account only for those changes which enhance reproduction; they cannot explain the origin or perpetuation of overdesigned systems that are advantageous largely in an organism's post-reproductive period.

Homology and Aphanisia

If two very different creatures have organs which possess an underlying structural similarity but serve different functions, these organs are said to be *homologous*. The human arm and the flipper of a seal, for example, have an internal bone structure that is similar even though one organ functions differently. Macroevolutionists believe that these homologous organs resulted from divergent evolution by which man and seal, for example, descended from common ancestry. They assume that the human arm, the leg of a dog, the whale's flipper, and the forelimb of a bat are all organically related.

Homologous organs fit just as well with the concept that the Designer used a certain plan in many animals because that particular scheme was efficient or utilitarian. Instead of appealing to common ancestry, appeal is made to a common Designer. In this monograph we concentrate on vestigial rather than homologous organs. It can be shown, however, that homologies also support the design interpretation because they are evidences of basic patterns or plans—see Howe (1971).

Homology, as it was originally defined by Richard Owen, has no phylogenetic significance and merely designates similarities without reference to ancestry—see Boyden (1947). DeBeer agreed that homology should not be used as a guide to phylogeny:

> It is now clear that the pride with which it was assumed that the inheritance of homologous structures from a common ancestor explained homology was misplaced; for such inheritance cannot be ascribed to identity of genes. The attempt to find 'homologous' genes, except in closely related species, has been given up as hopeless. DeBeer (1971:16)

Aphanisia, on the other hand, is the appearance during ontogeny of certain organs which become successively reabsorbed during embryological development until they disappear. These organs are useful during certain stages of development, but when they are no longer functional they are either reabsorbed or they drop off. Aphanisia occurs when the mammalian umbilical cord falls off as it is no longer needed or in the case of teeth in the jaw of a fetal baleen whale which are reabsorbed (to be discussed in section II). Such organs convey an understanding of an animal's individual development (ontogeny) but they do not portray its evolutionary development (phylogeny).

Aphanisic structures differ from rudimentary organs in that the former structure at first develops and is fully functional, only to be totally consumed or lost later, while the latter continue development in the young but later experience a partial reduction. A rudimentary structure remains at least present in the adult, although less functional—see Rensch (1959:225). K. S. Thomson (1988) has indicated that the concept of ontogeny recapitulating phylogeny (better known as the biogenetic law of Ernst Haeckel) supplies no evidence for macroevolution. Rusch (1969) showed that part of Haeckel's work on recapitulation was even fraudulent.

Some organs found in the developmental stages of the embryo still remain present in the adult stage but are less useful. These cannot be considered vestigial. Most organs which become smaller or disappear in childhood are known to be necessary or at least functional during certain developmental stages. When they become less useful or less important, they are "programmed out" by the genetic code. Their disappearance is evidence for design instead of support for their vestigial nature. The eyes of larval cave salamanders, for example, disappear during metamorphosis—see section II.

A. Thomson (1958:207) noted that many so-called vestigial organs are probably functional in the embryonic stage, yet are not normally important in the adult. They are necessary in certain stages of body construction and are thus similar to scaffolding that is needed in the building of a house, but is removed when the job is completed.

As an example he cited the notochord which is a simple skeletal rod present in adult lancelets and lampreys, both of which lack a true backbone. In the early development of the embryonic human there is also a notochord but it is transient, not being present in the adult. This ephemeral notochord in humans serves an important developmental role even though it is later replaced with a more functional structure, the backbone.

A. Thomson also noted that the so-called visceral pouches or "gill-clefts," which are actually "flexure folds" or "give points" of the human embryo:

> ... may have some present day developmental value, though only the first comes to much in the adult, where it forms the Eustachian tube from the ear passage to the back of the mouth. A. Thomson (1958:207)

Both aphanisia and homology are seen to fit the design model of origins.

The Problem of Purpose

A major temptation that anti-evolutionists face in counteracting the concept of useless organs is the desire to go beyond describing function, and to impute the "purpose" for an organ. It is difficult to specify the exact purpose of any organ because to do so implies knowing the mind of the Designer. In seeking purpose, for example, one might superficially and foolishly infer that the original design "purpose" of the nose bridge is to hold up one's eye glasses.

Clear function of most organs can be determined, however. One function of vitreous humor is to give a specific shape to the eyeball, a shape which guarantees that light coming into the eye will be bent to focus on the retina. Even with this statement we would be on shaky ground to infer that this is the eyeball's "main purpose." From our vantage point, we focus on functions; it is seldom possible for us to know with assurance the full "purpose" for which the Designer produced a given organ.

The Lack of Nascent Organs Is a Problem to Macroevolutionists

From the macroevolutionary model one might predict that some organs would be fully functional while many others would be functionless "leftovers" from previous evolutionary stages. Yet other structures would be expected to be in the process of evolving or improving their functionality—this includes both rudimentary organs and nascent organs. Examples of nascent organs are very few if not totally nonexistent.

The evolutionary assumptions about vestigial organs imply design and teleology. These assumptions are commonly held by many macroevolutionists who would otherwise disavow all teleological thought patterns or design ideology.

Vestigial Organs as a Test of Origins Predictions

To demonstrate that each of the so-called vestigial organs clearly has a function would falsify one of the original predictions of the macroevolultion model. On the other hand, believers in design would predict that each organ in the body is useful as part of its integrated plan.

Let us examine several structures still considered by many evolutionists to be without function. The predictive strength of the design and the macroevolution models can be evaluated by studying supposed examples of functionless organs.

PART II:
FUNCTIONS OF SPECIFIC ORGANS STILL BELIEVED TO BE USELESS VESTIGES

The Coccyx Defined as a Supposed Vestige

Humans differ from most primates in that they lack a tail. The lower primates have tails, and the apes, which are believed by many to be our closest relatives, likewise are tailless. The human coccyx (also called the *os coccyx*) was viewed by Drummond (1903) as a rudimentary tail left over from our distant past and therefore vestigial. The coccyx bones were interpreted as remnants of a structure which strongly linked humans to the lower primates.

Both D. Morris (1985) and Pansky (1975) saw the coccyx as all that yet remains of our primate tail. Cartmill *et al.* (1987:186) asserted that the coccygeus muscle and sacrospinous ligament which attach to the coccyx are vestiges of a "... powerful muscle that acts to tuck the tail down in a dog's body." Pinchot (1985:41) claimed that the coccyx is the only part of the skeleton without a function. The coccyx and associated structures were and still are beleved to be useless remnants of evolution.

The coccyx is composed of three to five (usually four) nodular pieces of fused vertebral bones at the lowest part of the vertebral column. There is some evidence that the coccyx in modern humans is one vertebra longer than it was in Neanderthals; but this difference may be merely a racial variation.

Contributions of The Coccyx

The coccyx is triangular in shape and attached to the bottom of the sacrum. Its name "coccyx" means cuckoo; it was named because of its resemblance to a cuckoo's bill—see Walker (1987:253). Because it is not connected to the ribs, the coccyx does not have pedicles, lamina, or spinous processes that are present on certain other vertebrae. The coccygeal vertebrae have only three transverse grooves which provide an attachment to the ventral sacrococcygeal ligaments and the *levatores ani*, two broad thin muscles which form part of the hammock-like floor of the pelvis. These muscles function as a single sheet which extends across the middle line, forming the principal part of the pelvic diaphragm and support for the rectum. The coccygeus muscle also helps to support the posterior organs of the pelvic floor, especially during blocked forced expiration, as in elimination.

The *coccygeus* muscle can draw the coccyx ventrally to give added support to the pelvic floor against abdominal pressure. It draws the coccyx forward after defecation. This muscle is inserted by its base into the margin of the coccyx and into the side of the last section of the sacrum. The coccygeus muscle consists of the *levator ani* and the *prirformis* which enclose the back part of the outlet of the pelvis.

In females, the coccygeus muscle draws the coccyx forward after it has been pressed back during parturition. Smith (1986:134) reported that the movements of the coccyx help to enlarge the birth canal during childbirth. The *levator ani* muscles constrict the lower end of both the rectum and the vagina, drawing the rectum both forward and upward—see Anthony (1963:411). Far from being remnants of muscles that pull the tail down in a dog, as Cartmill *et al.* (1987:186) and others claim, the small sling of muscles attached to the coccyx serves several functions.

On the left and right dorsal surfaces of the coccyx is located a row of tubercles called the "rudimentary articular processes." However, they are "rudimentary" only in the sense that they are smaller than the tubercles on the thoracic vertebrae. The larger first pair, the *coccygeal cornua*, articulate with the cornua of the sacrum and allow some movement. On the oppsite side are the openings called foramina—openings for the transmission of the dorsal division of the fifth sacral nerve. The narrow borders of the coccyx receive the attachment of the *sacrotuberous* and *sacrospinous* ligaments laterally for support of the bones, the coccygeus muscle ventrally, and the *gluteus maximus* muscle dorsally.

The oval surface of the coccyx base articulates with the sacrum. Gray (1966:130) pointed out that the rounded apex or lowest part of the coccyx is attached to the tendon of the *sphincter ani externus* and its movement can be bifid, meaning that it can be deflected to both sides, and thus make bowel movements possible. Also, Gray (1966: 130) discussed the *anococcygeal raphe* which is a narrow fibrous band that extends from the coccyx to the margin of the anus.

Citing an anatomy textbook, Scadding (1981) concluded this very succinctly by stating that several muscles and ligaments insert on the coccyx. Walker (1987:253) noted that it is the coccyx "... to which certain anal and perineal muscles attach." Weischnitzer (1978: 285) reported that the *iliococcygeus* muscle "... supports and raises the pelvic floor." He indicated that the iliococcygeus is inserted on terminal parts of the coccyx.

Without the coccyx and its attached muscle system, humans would need a radically different support system for their internal organs which would require numerous design changes in the human posterior. Concerning the coccyx and its importance, Allford concluded that:

> The posterior surfaces [of the coccyx] serve as attachments for the gluteus maximus muscle and the sphincter and externus muscles. The gluteus maximus muscle is essential for defecation and labor during childbirth. The sphincter ani externus muscle is needed to keep the anal canal and orifice closed. These are obviously very important functions. The interior surfaces of the coccygeal vertebrae also serve as important attachments for muscles that aid in the containment of feces within the rectum ... [as well as control of] defecation, and the expulsion of the fetus during labor. For these

important reasons, the coccyx can never be classified as a rudimentary or vestigial rudiment of our ancestors. Allford (1978:42)

Franks dealt with coccyx malfunction as follows:

> Individuals who injure the tail-bone may develop a painful condition called coccydynia. Removal of the coccyx presumably because it is thought to be nonessential seems to be a poor operation. I counsel my patients with tail-bone pain to resist removal of the coccyx if ever suggested. Franks (1988:24)

The coccyx is not the only support system of the internal organs; the diaphragm and other muscles also help fulfill this role. If the coccyx is surgically removed, enough surrounding supporting structures exist in adults so one can live fairly normally. The three to five small bones are obviously part of a larger support structure consisting of bones, cartilage, muscle, ligaments, and tendons, all of which participate.

Concerning surgery of the coccyx, Shute noted that the vestigial organ argument is not realistic:

> ... Take it away and patients complain; indeed the operation for its removal has time and again fallen into disrepute, only to be revived by some naive surgeon who really believes what the biologists have told him about this useless 'rudiment.' Shute (1961:40)

Reno argued that the coccyx need not be classed as a useless remnant of evolution. Her practical words illustrate the fact that the coccyx was often judged vestigial merely because of its position "The coccyx ... is merely the terminal portion of the backbone. After all, it does have to have an end!" Reno (1970:81)

Does The Human Embryo Have A Tail?

Asimov asserted that man's embryo has a tail:

> If there is any doubt that the coccyx represents a tail and not something else entirely, the answer lies in the study of the developing human embryo. In the early stages a small but distinct tail region is formed. By the eighth week of development it is gone, but its evanescent existence would seem to make it clear, that man descended from some creature with a tail, and that he still carries about with him, hidden below the skin, a last evidence of it. Asimov (1963:39)

Some years later Smith took a different view of the human embryonic "tail":

> ... although the human embryo has a short stub of a tail for a while and this is precisely similar to the short stubs that become tails in many other species, the human tail stub only forms the basis of the human coccyx. Mankind does not travel up the trunk of the animal tree with each embryo. ... Smith (1986:118).

Gould (1982:41) noted that at four weeks humans have a well-formed tail which is larger at that time than their legs. Shute (1961:40) added that although in its development, the human embryo appears tailed this is simply because ". . . there is disproportionate development of various parts of the fetal skeleton."

Are Some Human Babies Actually Born With A Tail?

At birth some human babies have a short "tail-like" growth called a "caudal appendage," located near the inferior end of the spinal column. While documenting the occurrence of such caudal appendages, Ledley stated the evolutionists' bold cliam about the supposed relationship of the caudal appendage to human origins:

> There is something seemingly unhuman about the presence on a human infant of a 'tail' like the tails found on other primates. It is incongruous; it violates our sense of anthropocentricity, and it raises issues that involve not only teratology and embryology but also our view of ourselves and our place in evolution. . . .
>
> To evolutionists the 'human tail' was an example of a 'reversion to a lower species' and an illustration of the doctrine that 'ontogeny recapitulates phylogeny' . . .
>
> The human tail serves as an example of modern concepts of ontogeny and phylogeny and presents a striking clinical confrontation with the reality of evolution. . . .
>
> Even those who are familiar with the literature that defined our place in nature—from Darwin's *The Descent of Man* to Wilson's *On Human Nature*—are rarely confronted with the relation between human beings and their primitive ancestors on a daily basis. The caudal appendage brings this reality to the fore and makes it tangible and inescapable. Ledley (1982:1212, 1215)

The brief research portion of Ledley's paper (1982:1212) concerned the case report of a 7-pound baby that was born with a caudal appendage 2 inches in length. Shortly after it was born the child was transferred to Children's Hospital Medical Center in Boston where doctors removed the growth. Ledley related that it was a ". . . well-formed caudal appendage" located near the end of the baby's spine; ". . . it was covered by skin of normal texture and had a soft fibrous consistency." Ledley also noted that there were no vertebrae or even cartilaginous elements in the so-called "caudal appendage." Ledley included a helpful review of caudal appendage research. Such cases have been noted throughout history, but very few have been scientifically documented. The rest of Ledley's paper consisted of a bold defense of macroevolution involving ontogeny and comparative embryology.

We do not intend to discuss the evolutionary concept that an individual retraces his evolution during his embryological development; *viz.*, "ontogeny recapitulates phylogeny." It will be sufficient to note that some embryologists have totally rejected this idea as an appealing but naive and mistaken view of embryogenesis:

> I wonder whether the phrase 'ontogeny recapitulates phylogeny' would so persistently have fascinated biologists, or so long have survived among the debris of half forgotten science that we all retain from high school, if it were not rather euphonious. Would something like 'development repeats evolutinary history' have worn so well? K. S. Thomson (1988)

K. S. Thomson (1988) also asserted that the recapitulation concept has little if any meaning in modern biology; he viewed it to be a dead concept. In addition to demonstrating that Haeckel's paradigm is totally inadequate, Rusch (1969) showed that some of Haeckel's drawings purporting to demonstrate embryonic recapitulation were fraudulent. Even Gould (1982:41), the reviewer of Ledley's paper, noted that ". . . the theory of recapitulation died more than fifty years ago."

Remine and an anonymous coauthor from the University of Minnesota analyzed Ledley's findings shortly after the report was published. Their pointed critique of Ledley's evolutionary thesis speaks for itself:

> In evaluating this case report it may be noted firstly that the caudal appendage is not connected to the vertebral column as are the tails of other vertebrates. In addition, the appendage is not even in line with the vertebral column but is 1.5 cm to the right of the midline. Secondly, the appendage contains no bony structures as do the tails of all other vertebrates. These two points support the interpretation that this appendage is not a "true tail" but is likely a dermal (skin) remnant of the fetal ectoderm germ layer located by chance in the caudal region. [ReMine here quoted Ledley to show that these caudal appendages of certain human babies are very different than true tails in other vertebrates.]
>
> Many evolutionists view the appendage as tail-like enough to be interpreted as evidence of man's primitive evolutionary ancestry. This interpretation has two drawbacks. One drawback is that there are good reasons, as given above, why the appendage may not be interpreted as a true tail. Secondly, there is no well established genetic mechanism to account for the preservation of the structural elements necessary for tail formation in the human genome.
>
> Creationists may view the appendage as a structural variant of developmental origin rather than as a 'tail.' ReMine (1982:8)

Ledley himself (1982) admitted that the so-called caudal appendage may be nothing more than a dermal appendage which by chance occurred in that position. Reno noted that one explanation of these abnormal caudal appendages is that each is merely a birth abnormality:

Could not this be the result of a deranged process taking place during embryologic development? The normal process is sometimes altered and as a result we see Siamese twins, cleft palates and harelips. No on would argue that these were once normal conditions in a remote ancestor. A 'tail' could be such an anomaly. Reno (1970:86).

See also Rijsbosch (1960 and 1977) and Gish (1983) for further discussion of this idea that the caudal appendage may be only one of many birth abnormalities.

The Tonsils and Adenoids Described

Other organs which long have been considered vestigial include the tonsils and adenoids. The tonsils are two lumps of lymphatic tissue which lie on both sides of the throat directly behind the tongue. The tonsils are composed of three sets of lymphoid tissues. The first of these is the palatine tonsils which are often referred to simply as "the tonsils." They are two oval masses of lymphoid tissue attached to the side wall at the back of the mouth between the anterior pillar, called the palatoglossal arch, and the posterior pillar, known as the palatopharyngeal arch.

The second tissue components of this tonsil ring are the nasopharyngeal tonsils which are commonly called the adenoids. They are a mass of lymphoid tissue located on the nasopharynx and extending from the roof of the nasopharynx posteriorly as far as the free edge of the soft palate— the posterior dorsal wall of the pharynx.

The last section of the ring contains the lingual tonsils, which consist of two masses of lymphoid tissue found on the dorsum of the tongue. They extend from the vallate papillae of the tongue all the way to the epiglottis.

The Vestigial Label and Tonsil Surgery

The assumption that the tonsils are vestigial has been one reason for the frequency of tonsillectomies in the past. In many cases when it was assumed that tonsillitis existed, the problem was nothing more than some type of throat infection which may have occurred regardless or whether the tonsils were present or not. When the throat is irritated for any reason, the tonsils also become irritated, but only in response to the nearby throat infection. Removal of the tonsils was usually unrelated to the cause of the infection.

The tonsils were first suspected as the cause of health problems when a connection was noticed between the size of the tonsils and respiratory infections. When children have the greatest severity of colds, tonsils swell; when they have their least severity, the tonsils are far smaller. It was thus believed that the tonsils were of no use and could cause problems. Many tonsillectomies were performed for no other reason than the belief that since they must come out sooner or later, it was better to remove them when the patient was younger, when the body could endure surgery better. In recent years, however, researchers have demonstrated the function of both tonsils and adenoids. As a result of these newer data, most doctors are now reluctant to remove either the tonsils or the adenoids.

In the 1930's over half of all children had their tonsils and adenoids removed. In 1969 19.5 out of every 1,000 children under the age of nine had undergone a tonsillectomy. By 1971 the frequency had dropped to only 14.8 per 1,000, with the percentage continuing to decrease in subsequent years. Most medical authorities now actively discourage tonsillectomies—see Bolande (1969), Eden (1977), Galton (1976), Katz (1972), and Lipton (1962). Many agree with Wooley, chairman of the department of pediatrics at Wayne State University, who was quoted in Katz:

> If there are one million tonsillectomies done in the United States, there are 999,000 that don't need doing. Katz (1972:1)

Among the first medical doctors seriously to question the wisdom of tonsillectomies was Albert Kaiser. For 10 years he kept complete records of the illnesses of 5,000 children. They were divided into two groups—those who had tonsils removed and those who did not. According to Galton, Kaiser found:

> ... no significant difference between the two groups in the number of colds, sore throats and other upper respiratory infections. Galton (1976:26)

In fact, a large body of developing evidence suggests that removal of the tonsils may actually weaken the child's resistance to certain infections and diseases in general. Workers in the New York Department of Cancer Control concluded that:

> ... people who have had tonsillectomies are nearly three times as likely to develop Hodgkin's disease, a form of cancer that attacks the lymphoid tissue. Galton (1976:26-27).

> Part of this increased susceptibility may result from some psychological repercussions of the operation. Lipton (1962).

The tonsils are important to young people in helping to establish the body's defense mechanism which produces disease-fighting antibodies. Once these defense mechanisms are developed, the tonsil shrinks to almost nothing in adults, and other organs take over this function—see Gross (1966) and Hall (1941). Many researchers conclude that because tonsils are larger in children than in adults, the tonsils are important in the growth of the whole immunological system—Jacob et al. (1982). Williams (1970) reported general agreement among doctors that a tonsillectomy should be performed only when the tonsils themselves become chronically infected and, being no longer a barrier to infections they actually become a source of disease. Some doctors go even further, suggesting that there is seldom a need to remove the tonsils even after repeated infections because antibiotics are readily available. Eden concluded that:

> The location of the tonsils and adenoids allows them to act as a trap and firstline defense against inhaled or ingested bacteria and viruses. The tonsils and adenoids are made up of lymphoid tissue which manufactures antibodies against invading diseases. Therefore, unless there is an important and specific reason to have the operation, it is better to leave the tonsils and adenoids in place. Eden (1977:24)

This current view is in remarkable contrast to the outlook promoted in 1957. In a book written to allay children's fears of hospitals, Chase (1957) began:

> Steve was sick in bed with a cold. 'Why do I have so many colds?' he asked his Mommy. . . . 'Maybe it's your tonsils that are giving you so many colds.' 'What are tonsils?' Steve asked. 'Tonsils are two little things in the back of our throats,' Mommy said. 'When children are little, their tonsils help to keep them well, but when they grow older—like you, Steve—tonsils very often cause colds and sore throats. Then they're not needed anymore, so the doctor takes them out.' . . . [at the doctor's office] 'Well,' said the doctor 'Just as I thought. Those tonsils. We'd better take them out.' Chase (1957:1ff)

Although removal of tonsils obviously eliminates tonsillitis (the inflammation of the tonsils) it may significantly increase the incidence of strep throat or even Hodgkin's disease—Vianna *et al.* (1972). The results of empirical research on the value of tonsillectomies in preventing infection:

> . . . demonstrate that the tonsillectomy is of little benefit after the age of eight when the child's natural defenses have already made him immune to many infections. Katz (1972).

Tonsil Functions Now Known

It is now generally accepted that the tonsils are part of the adult body's lymphatic system, the function of which is filtering out and fighting disease organisms—Syzmanowski as quoted in Katz (1972); see also Gross (1966), Jacob *et al.* (1978), and Culp (1975). Jacob *et al.* (1978:714) concluded that the tonsils:

> . . . form a ring of lymphoid tissue . . . [that guards] . . . the entrance of the alimentary and respiratory tracts from bacterial invasion.

Katz (1973:1) reported that tonsils provided protection from ". . . exposure to bacteria and viruses . . . [which cause] . . . colds and sore throats." He also remarked that removing the tonsils will not lessen the number of infections but may actually increase them.

A Description of the Vermiform Appendix

The lower right end of the large intestine terminates somewhat abruptly with the cecum (also spelled caecum). The small intestine empties into the large intestine above the floor of the cecum. The entrance into the large intestine is controlled by a valve.

Connected to the cecum is the vermiform appendix which is a small, narrow, worm-shaped tube. The human appendix can vary in length from 19 to almost 200 millimeters although its average length is slightly over 76 mm (about three inches long). Morrison (1967: 252).

The name "vermiform" means "wormlike" and "appendix" means "added to." The vermiform appendix is also called the processus vermiformis. At one time it was called the *Appendix Vermiformis Cici* which is still its correct name, according to *Nomina Anatomica*.

The appendix has been long regarded as a vestigial organ and probably still is the most commonly cited example—see Moody (1953), Birdsell (1972), and Drummond (1903). Most early workers stated emphatically, as did R. Morris (1895), that it ". . . has no function." Jordan and Kellogg concluded that:

> Since man has been walking on two feet, the appendix has lost whatever function it may have had in primitive times. Such an organ is a vestigial one. Jordan and Kellogg (1908:178)

Macroevolutionists have proposed that humans descended from an ancestor that had a much larger cecum. They asserted that this large cecum decreased in size and lost its digestive function to produce the appendix and the much smaller cecum of modern man. The appendix is still cited in many biology texts as the best example of a vestigial organ—see Raven and Johnson (1988:322) and Mader (1988:510).

Asimov wrote that:

> In man what is left of the caecum (a vestige perhaps of herbivorous ancestors) is of no particular use and can actually be a source of trouble . . . [it is] a further remnant of a once sizeable and usable caecum. Asimov (1963:243)

Brum and McKane (1989:498, 500) asserted that, "The human appendix is a degenerated cecum . . . one of the useless relics of once useful ancestral structures." Concerning the supposed useless nature of the appendix, Smith (1986:465) bluntly stated that: "No one knows the purpose of the appendix."

Problems With the Appendix

Cartmill *et al.* described acute appendicitis:

> . . . an acute infection may cause it to rupture when the walls of the cecum contract, thus spilling intestinal contents and bacteria into the abdominl celom. Before antibiotics, rupture of the appendix ordinarily resulted in a fatal celomic infection (peritonitis) and rapid death. Cartmill *et al.* (1987:136)

Thus one of the main reasons why the appendix was viewed as useless was that no clear adverse effects resulted from its removal. But as Artist (1969) noted, and as we have previously discussed, it is foolish to claim that an organ is vestigial just because it can be removed from a large sample of people with no apparent ill effects.

It must be remembered that most biologists refrain from calling an organ vestigial if that organ has some function—even a non-vital function. If it can be shown to play any role, the organ in question does not qualify as "vestigial."

Because the appendix and cecum together form a blind sac, they fill easily and empty slugglishly. Consequently, materials may remain in them for considerable periods of time. Hard or rough substances not absorbed in the intestine may become trapped in the appendix, later to be digested by enzyme action. Extremely hard or rough substances may irritate the inner walls of the appendix, possible predisposing it to bacterial growth. A resulting inflammation may produce appendicitis. Because of this, Drummond (1903:95) wrote that the appendix is ". . . a structure which is not only of no use to man now but a veritable death trap." Looking at this problem of appendicitis from a different and lighter perspective, Romer and Parsons suggested that the appendix does have an economic function:

> Its major importance would appear to be the financial support of the surgical profession. Romer and Parsons (1986:389)

The Taxonomic Distribution of Appendices Confounds Phylogeny

According to the concept of neo-Darwinian macroevolutionism, one ought to find a series of organs graded in size from large and useful (like the cecum in the rabbit) to small and vestigial in animals that are similar to mankind. No such graded series is found. Among the primates an appendix is present in certain lemurs, humans, and four anthropoid apes; yet it is absent in monkeys—see Strauss (1947). Weichert and Presch (1975:268), Davidheiser (1969:235) noted that the appendix is scattered in widely separated taxomonic groups such as: the great apes, a few rodents, some civents, and (of course) *Homo sapiens*.

If these data were used to produce phylogenies, they would support the conclusion that sometimes animals lower on the supposed tree of evolution have evolved organs to a higher degree than the "higher" animals. If total absence of an appendix were a token of advancement, the old and new world monkeys should be considered more highly evolved than either mankind (or than the lemurs), a bizarre conclusion— see Bierman (1968:118).

The data would also support the conclusion that evolution repeatedly converted part of the cecum into an appendix independently along several different phylogenetic lines, an unlikely series of events that evolutionists call "parallel" or "convergent" evolution.

Some macroevolutionists also argue that the human appendix is an evolutionary throwback resulting from reactivation of dormant genes more typical of our distant evolutionary ancestors—a theoretical situation that macroevolutionists call "atavism." But the idea that the appendix is an atavistic organ has been largely discredited. Bergman (1990).

If natural selection were working to reduce the cecum one would expect to find a series of primate forms in which the cecum is reduced in size and ultimately eliminated. The fact that the appendix has not been altogether eliminated supports the belief that it has some function. As Davidheiser concluded:

> There is no pattern of distribution of this organ among the different sorts of animals such as would be expected if it had once been a prominent part of the cecum and then gradually become vestigial as evolving animals become diverse. Davidheiser (1969:236)

The presence or absence of the appendix is mixed in both carnivorous and omnivorous animals. This spotty pattern of distribution indicates that, although the cecum digests cellulose in rabbits, the appendix plays different roles in humans and other animals which possess it.

Another possible evolutionary explanation is that an appendix was highly detrimental to the survival of certain animals and was for this reason selected out of their lineage. None of these evolutionary explanations of the taxonomic data is either feasible or supported by the evidence; all are *post-hoc* arguments and hence not scientific.

The Cecum, Cellulose, and The Appendix

Cellulose is a fibrous part of plant food which cannot be digested by the enzymes secreted in the human digestive tract or in the tract of other animals. Cellulose digestion can occur as a result of cellulose-digesting microorganisms in the digestive tract. Even in humans some cellulose digestion can occur as a result of the activity of such microbes, but in such animals as the cow, large quantities of cellulose are digested bacteriologically.

Cellulose is known to be important in the human diet but not as a nutrient. It forms a small percentage of the human feces and contributes to its bulk. Bulk is important in stimulating the lining of the intestines to induce peristalsis. Nutritionists have repeatedly stressed the importance of fiber which provides bulk or roughage, especially that which is found in fruits, vegetables, and whole grains. Lack of roughage is sometimes a problem because much of it is processed out of food; constipation heads the list of resulting complications. Roughage retains water which facilitates the removal of waste from the system. Without enough liquid, the food becomes bound up within the intestinal tract. Many laxatives contain a type of cellulose roughage as their foremost ingredient.

In herbivores like the rabbit, the appendix is ". . . particularly well developed," and therefore quite useful—see Kluge (1977:301). In these animals both the appendix and the cecum are large, pocket-like structures at the junction of the small and large intestines—see Kent (1978:250). Bacteria capable of digesting cellulose live in the rabbit's cecum. Cellulose must be retained in the pocket long enough to be chemically changed into soluble materials which can be absorbed by the large intestine.

Macroevolutionists believe that the human cecum was originally much larger and became reduced in size, changing to an appendix, because man's ancestors slowly adapted to a different diet and no longer needed this organ. Most animals whose diet is primarily carnivorous have an appendix that is much smaller than the corresponding cecum of herbivores. Kluge (1977:301). But we know that disuse alone would not have caused the cecum to become progressively reduced in size to become a mere appendix. The Lamarckian concept of acquired characteristics has been abandoned because we now know that organs do not change in size from generation to generation as a function of use or disuse.

Macroevolutionists of the neo-Darwinian variety would argue that it was not disuse, but selection which converted a large, cellulose-digesting, cecum into a smaller cecum plus vestigial appendix. It is not clear in this selection model how a highly functional cecum which equipped an ancestral organism to house cellulose-digesting organisms would gradually decrease and all but vanish.

The Appendix, Antibodies, and Post-Radiation Survival

Clark (1934:205) foresaw that the rich blood supply in the appendix would show it to be functional. Maisel (1966) as well as Bloom and Fawcett (1975) concluded that the appendix, as part of the immune system, seems to function in the production of antibodies.

One of the more important nondigestive roles played by the appendix was discovered in the late 1950's and early 1960's by Sussdorf (1959), (1960), (1962), and (1974). He noted that the appendix helps in fighting the effects of post-radiation infection—see Davis (1960). After irradiation, the body's ability to manufacture antibodies is impaired to the extent that infections can sometimes run rampant. Death after radiation overdose is usually not directly caused by the radiation, but by subsequent infections.

During embryologic development the spleen modifies lymphatic stem cells coming from the fetal liver so they become B lymphocytes which enter the blood circulation. Antigens then stimulate B lymphocytes to become plasma cells which, in turn, generate antibody molecules.

Sussdorf (1959) (1960) found that if the appendix is covered with a lead shield when rabbits are exposed to X-rays, white pulp and hemolysin production in the spleen are enhanced after irradiation compared to control rabbits that did not have the appendix shielded. This is because of the presence of the lymphoid tissue in the appendix. When it is undamaged, it can help restore antibody production in the spleen.

If radiation damage reaches a certain level, antibody production in the spleen is temporarily impaired. After radiation, lymphoid cells (as those which might exist in the appendix if it had been shielded) migrate to the impaired spleen. There they manufacture antibodies until the spleen can recover enough to take over again. Lack of an appendix may seriously increase the danger of problems occurring after radiation exposure.

Hanaoka *et al.* (1970) irradiated rabbits that had their appendix and bone marrow shielded and then injected such rabbits with bovine gamma globulin. From their detailed studies they concluded that the appendix participates in antibody production but cannot complete the task by itself.

Ozer and Waksman (1970) found that irradiation together with an appendectomy completely inhibits the spleen. If a rabbit is given whole-body irradiation and an appendectomy, however, shielding the bone marrow and reinjecting with appendiceal cells brings about restoration of the immune response. These results support the conclusion that the bone marrow in conjunction with the appendix enables the rabbit to produce antibodies and to restore splenic activity.

The Appendix Has Lymphatic Functions

In their reviews of the literature, Klotz (1970:134) and Williams (1970) commented on the well-known fact that the appendix is rich in lymphoid tissue and proposed that it probably helps protect the human body against infection, especially during the early years of life. Because the appendix is in fact relatively large and conspicuous during embryological development, it is likely to be very important during this stage of life.

Based on the structure of man's appendix, Dawson (1978:90) concluded that it is a reasonable candidate for some role in the body's immunological system. Lankford wrote these pertinent words concerning theories about the function of the appendix:

> Two theories exist concerning the function of the appendix. One long-held theory is that the appendix is a non-functional structure that serves only to cause appendicitis. A newer theory is that the lymphatic tissue in the appendix acts to filter out bacteria, like Peyer's Patches and other lymph nodes. Lankford (1976:632)

Pansky (1975:430) likened the appendix to an "abdominal tonsil" because of the large amount of lymphoid tissue present—see also Singer and Hilgard (1978:257-258), Warrick (1969:191), and Gray (1985:899, 1481, 1487).

The appendix, as is true of all gut tissue, contains a large number of lumphatic nodules. Walker (1987:564, 646). Bloom and Fawcett (1975:673) reported that the appendix "... wall is thickened by an extensive development of lymphoid tissue which forms an almost continuous layer of large and small lymphatic nodules." The appendix lymphatic tissue is similar to that in the tonsils. Situated near the junction of the small intestine and the colon, the appendix appears to protect the intestines from infection in the cecum region where the colon begins. The antibodies would be manufactured close to the organs where they are used such as the entire gut lining. Cartmill *et al.* stated that:

The human appendix has masses of lymphatic tissue in its walls and seems to provide a local defense against infection from microorganisms in the colon. Cartmill *et al.* (1987:135)

Results from experimental studies with rabbits spurred Elves (1972: 173-174) to conclude that: ". . . the appendix may be a central lymphoid organ as well as the thymus." Here Elves was reporting on studies by Archer *et al.* (1964a and 1964b) in which thymectomized newborn rabbits showed a transitory depletion of lymphoid tissues which returned to normal by nine weeks of age.

From the foregoing results it was concluded that besides the thymus, there must be another source of lymphocytes in neonatal rabbits. Archer *et al.* (1964a and 1964b) further noted that recovery after irradiation did not occur by nine weeks if the appendix was also removed. Elves (1972: 174) concluded that the appendix has an important lymphatic function.

More recently Kawanishi (1987) showed that human lymphoid cells in the appendix are immunologically functional as T helper cells and antibody-producing B cells, making IgA molecules in response to immunological challenges. He noted that:

> This responsiveness to exogenous stimuli may play an important role in gut mucosal immune responsiveness. Kawanishi (1987:19).

Concerning the functionality of the appendix, Kawanishi penned these telling words:

> The human appendix, long considered only an accessory rudimentary organ, could possess a similar antigen uptake role prior to replacement by fibrosed tissue after repeated subclinical infections, or at least in early childhood when it is most prominent. Kawanishi (1987:19)

The appendix is also rich in argentaffin cells which can be identified with the use of silver salt staining. The function of these cells has long been obscure, but evidence suggests that they may be involved with endocrine gland function—see Marti-Ibanez (1970:240) and Banks (1981: 390). In light of the foregoing discussion, the appendix should be removed from the list of vestigial organs since it is a highly functional part of the immunological and endocrine systems.

A Possible Tie Between Cancer and The Absence of the Appendix
The appendix may play some role in cancer prevention:

> Dr. Howard R. Bierman . . . studied several hundred patients with leukemia, Hodgkin's disease, cancer of the colon and cancer of the ovaries. He found that 84% [of his sample] had [their] appendix removed . . . In a control group without cancer, only 25% had it removed. Culp (1975:65)

The above data merely indicate correlation and do not show causality. The possible role of the appendix in preventing some cancers is still controversial.

Bierman himself (1968:109) had concluded that the appendix may be an immunologic organ whose premature removal during its functional period permits leukemia and other related forms of cancer to begin their development. Bierman and his co-workers realized that lymphoid tissue located on the walls of the appendix may secrete antibodies which protect the body against various viral agents. In 1968 (pp. 109-118) Bierman noted that persons without an appendix were significantly more likely than those having an appendix to develop neoplastic diseases as a whole, including lymphoma, leukemia, and Hodgkin's disease.

Appendectomies and Origins

If the appendix becomes infected, it may increase the likelihood of death. But the same is true of any gland that becomes infected. Furthermore, appendicitis often occurs after the childbearing years, and in those cases would not substantially affect reproduction rates. This would reduce the speed at which it would be selected out, if it were truly useless. What is needed as support for evolutionism is evidence that animals that do not now possess an appendix once did. Such evidence is lacking.

Dawson presented a number of hypotheses as to the function of the human appendix. For example she assumed that:

> ... gut-associated lymphoid tissue may be associated with bacterial infection, since gut bacteria are probably the earliest bacteria encountered (even 'germ-free' animals encounter dead bacteria in their food); or it may be associated with the removal of mutated cells, since gut-lining cells are rapid dividers and so prone to mutation. Dawson (1978:90)

Dawson was aware of the obvious fact that:

> ... one cannot perform removal experiments of gut-associated lymphoid tissue on newborn humans to answer these queries, but one can carry out a survey to try to relate the absence of an appendix to infection. Dawson (1978:90)

Dawson attempted such a survey, but she encountered several problems involving small sample size and difficulty in obtaining reliable patient histories of vaccinations, tonsillectomies and general health problems. In addition, the experiment was difficult to control for a number of other reasons. Nonetheless, Dawson (1978) concluded that several relationships may exist between absence of an appendix, and subsequent infections.

Also emptying into the lumen of the appendix are the crypts of Lieberkuhn—Bloom and Fawcett (1975); Culp (1975). These glands contain goblet cells that produce a mucous lubricant which is also found in the lining of the small intestine and the colon. After an appendectomy one may suffer from constipation, according to Culp (1975), possibly related to the production of less mucus. It takes time for other areas of the intestine to compensate even though the total loss of tissue in an appendectomy is slight.

In light of the data reviewed here, only preconceived anticreationist notions could cause one to believe that the appendix is vestigial in *Homo sapiens*.

The vermiform appendix is not a useless vestige, according to Cartmill et al.:

> People sometimes speak of it as a vestigial organ, as though it were a useless remnant of a long cecum like that of a rabbit. *It is not* [emphasis ours] Cartmill *et al.* (1987:136)

And Franks concluded that:

> The appendix is able to sample the bowel contents and form antibodies. It is in a very beautiful location to do this. Of course, like the tonsils it sometimes falls prey to infection and requires removal. Again, God has built a fail-safe mechanism so that we can get along without the appendix. There are hundreds of lymphatic glands in the mesentery . . . Franks (1968:24)

Bierman's view was that "The vermiform appendix in man is not a functionless vestigial structure . . ." (1968:118).

The Thymus

The thymus gland is an example of an important organ which was long judged vestigial and, even was thought to be harmful if it became enlarged. Clayton (1983) noted that an oversized thymus was routinely irradiated in bygone years to shrink it. Through follow-up studies it was found later that, instead of helping the patient, such radiation treatment resulted in abnormal growth and a higher level of infectious diseases which persisted longer than normally.

Now labeled the "master gland" of the body's intricate immunity system, the thymus is known to play key roles in directing the development of a functioning adult immunologic system. Maisel reported this changed view of the thymus as follows:

> Modern physicians came to regard it, like the appendix, as a useless, vestigial organ which has lost its original purpose . . . In the last few years, however . . . a small band of [scientists] . . . has cracked the thymus engima. These men have proved that, far from being useless, the thymus is really the master gland that regulates the intricate immunity system which protects us against infectious diseases. Thanks to these discoveries, scores of researchers are now pursuing new and highly promising lines of attack against a wide range of major diseases, from arthritis to cancer. Others are

coming closer to the successful life-saving transplantation of entire organs. Maisel (1966:229)

Description of the Thymus

The thymus, a lympho-epithelial organ consisting of two pyramidal-shaped lobes connected by an isthmus, is located below the larynx and behind the sternum in the mediastinum—Greisheimer and Wideman (1972). It is surrounded by a capsule from which trabeculae extend inward, dividing it into several lobules which are functional units called "follicles."

The main body or cortex of the thymus is densely packed with small lymphocytes surrounded by epithelial-reticular cells. The lymphocytes, or thymic cells, which are produced in the cortex, leave it by way of the medulla—see Guyton (1966:139). The medulla is more vascular than the cortex, and its epithelial-reticular cells outnumber the lymphocytes.

The thymus is supplied with blood from the internal thoracic artery and the inferior thyroid artery. It receives some branches of the vagus nerve and the lateral cervical ganglia.

Functions of the Thymus

Greisheimer and Wideman present various thymus functions:

> The thymus produces lymphocytes, plasma cells and myelocytes. It is concerned with immunity. The best evidence for internal secretion is derived from experiments in which grafts of the thymus are placed in capsules with such small pores that cells cannot get out, yet the grafts are effective in preventing the [normal] effects of [the] removal of the thymus in young animals. The lymphocytes in the graft die, but the epithelial cells live . . . Greisheimer and Wideman (1972: 572-573)

Thymus-generated lymphocytes are important in defending against disease by responding to foreign proteins such as those in bacterial cell walls. In response to such antigens, lymphocytes also can develop into cells that produce antibody molecules which help the body kill microbes. Cooper et al. (1966) indicated that the lymphoid system is composed of functionally distinctive cell populations, each with a separate embryologic influence. The "thymus-dependent" system of lymphocytes mediates cellular immune responses such as delayed hypersensitivity allograft rejection, and reaction to bacteria—see Kretschmer et al. (1968).

Greisheimer and Wideman (1972) observed that in adults the thymus shrinks and is not nearly as important as it was in childhood. For this reason it was viewed for some time as an unimportant organ. But, it has been found that if the thymus is removed early in life, before the immunological system has been established, the entire system will fail to develop properly. Even after the immunological system is well developed, the effects of a thymectomy are still important, especially after the occurrence of crises affecting the immunological system. For this reason, Klotz (1970:135) concluded that:

The thymus is necessary not only for establishing normal immunological potential during development, but also for restoring such potential after it has been destroyed or damaged and possibly for maintaining it as it becomes depleted with time.

In his research at the University of Minnesota, Good (1973) found that patients whose thymus was destroyed by a benign tumor suffered from an acquired lack of gamma globulin. The result is both a lack of resistance, and an increased susceptibility, to diseases such as pneumonia. Thymectomy in newborn rabbits resulted in their total inability to manufacture antibodies and normal lymphocytes—Good (1973).

In research aimed at finding out how the thymus works, Levey (1964) concluded that it is the area of development for lymphocytes which, in turn, are sent out as "colonists" to mature and multiply in the spleen and lymph nodes. Allford (1978:48) noted that in rabbits thymectomy coupled with appendectomy caused a striking defect in antibody response in comparison to rabbits who underwent thymectomy alone. Since the human appendix also has lymphoid tissue, it is possible that the appendix and thymus gland cooperate in developing the body's immunological defenses.

In summary, the primary function of the thymus is a place of maturation for the small, white blood cells called lymphocytes, which are then sent to the spleen and the lymph nodes, where they mature and multiply. The thymus serves throughout life as a stimulus to spleen and lymph nodes in the manufacture of lymphocytes–see Maisel (1966). Whole books have been written since the 1960's about the immunological functions of the thymus—see Wolstenholme and Porter (1966), Defendi and Metcalf (1964), and Luckey (1973).

Description of The Pineal Gland—
Another Supposed Vestigial Organ

The pineal body is a cone-shaped gland that projects over the midbrain and lies in a groove in the center of what specialists call the superior colliculi of the quadrigeminal bodies. The pineal gland is attached to the midbrain by a median stalk, the base of which is hollowed out to form what is known as the pineal recess. Because the pineal body is derived from the roof of the diencephalon portion of the brain, it is also called the ephiphysis.

The pineal body contains ephithelioid cells arranged in cords and follicles, which are surrounded by blood vessels and interstitial cells. The epithelioid cells have large nuclei that are infolded or lobulated. The bulk of the organ is made of pinealocytes which have long turtuous processes that extend radially from the follicles and cords and terminate in bulb-shaped swellings. Greisheimer and Widemand (1972:571) stated that the cytoplasm of certain pineal gland cells ". . . contains free ribosomes and short vesicles of an atypical non-granular endoplasmic reticulum." The abundant tubules and vesicles of a non-granular endoplasmic reticulum are clear evidence that the pinealocytes are metabolically active.

The pineal gland was long considered "... a rather useless appendage left over from a lower form of life" as Yolles (1966:77) reported—see also Lull (1932:666). At one time it was thought to be a "vestigial third eye" because in certain animals it is located between the eyes and has photoreceptive cells. Yolles (1966:77) related an early idea that "... the pineal gland was all that remained in the higher vertebrates of the median eye which existed in primitive arthropods." The pineal gland evidently does function as a light sensing device in the lancelet, a small fish-like sea animal. Some workers still propose that the pineal gland was the evolutionary precursor of the modern vertebrate eye—see J. A. Miller (1985).

Light Is Shed on The Pineal Gland's Functions

Workers have found that the pineal gland is far from useless. Yolles concluded that it has hormonal functions:

> Scientists are closing in on a *mystery gland* of the human body, *the last organ for which no function has been known*. It is turning out to be a lively performer with a prominent role in the vital hormone-producing endocrine system ... Medical science is now finding what nature really intended by placing a pea-sized organ in the middle of the head. [Emphasis ours.] Yolles (1966:77)

The pineal gland was shown to play a role in reproduction by Blask:

> Over the past fifteen years a voluminous literature has accumulated which unequivocally establishes a nexus between the gland and the reproductive system in mammals. It has long been known that reduction in the amount of light reaching the eyes stimulates this small gland to synthesize and secrete an anti-gonadotrophic hormone(s) which results in marked attenuation of virtually all aspects of reproductive physiology. The pineal gland is a true neuroendocrine transducer and as such is able to convert, through rather complex neuronal circuitry, a photic-neural input into an anti-gonadrotrophic hormonal output. Blask (1982:124)

Researchers at the National Institute of Mental Health found that the pineal gland is a very active member of the body's network of endocrine glands, especially during certain growth stages. A. Thompson stated that:

> It seems a sad irony that modern anatomists regarded as vestigial the organ which Descartes regarded as 'the seat of the soul.' A. Thompson (1958:208)

Descartes imagined that the pineal gland was capable of secreting "animal spirit" which he believed to activate nerves—see Arendt (1985:36-38). She indicated that the writing of Descartes showed "astonishing intuition" because Descartes implied that the pineal gland was controlled by messages from the eyes. Additional data on pineal gland functions are found in Wurtman *et al.* (1968).

The Pineal Gland and Melatonin Production

The pineal gland's most commonly mentioned function is its role in producing the hormone *melatonin*—Erzin *et al.* (1973:10) and Greiner and Chan (1978:83-84). Among melatonin's functions is that of regulation of the estrus cycle. Cells in the pineal gland produce melatonin from serotonin through the catalytic action of hydroxyindole-o-methyl transferase—see Greisheimer and Wideman (1972) and Turner (1966:479).

The relationship between the pineal gland and light has brought about a wide range of speculation, most notably the effect of light upon reproduction and other sexual phenomena in both humans and animals. Melatonin regulates the production of anti-gonadotropin hormones which in turn play a part in retardation of gonadal development by blocking the effects of gonadotropic hormones. Destruction or damage to the pineal gland leads to precocious puberty in males. On the other hand, if the pineal gland is overactive, puberty is delayed. The pineal gland is the primary controller of the timing of the onset of puberty which is a very important developmental function. Almost any recent textbook on hormones or endocrinology contains several pages or even whole chapters that are devoted to the pineal gland and its regulatory hormone, melatonin.

An understanding of the exact function of melatonin has been expedited by sensitive analytical techniques which demonstrate the presence of melatonin in the blood, urine, and cerebral spinal fluid of humans as well as in the pineal gland—see Greiner and Chan (1978) and Reiter (1977). Interestingly, the level of melatonin is related to day-night cycles. During nocturnal periods, blood and urine levels of melatonin increase in both sexes; during daytime hours the level is at its lowest—Arendt (1985). Blask (1982:125) concluded that certain aspects of pineal function in humans respond to changes in lighting. Brainard noted this effect of light by saying that light talks to the brain via the pineal gland—Begley and Cook (1985:64).

Melatonin can help jet lag in transatlantic flights. Melatonin was given travelers at 6 p.m. for several days before a flight from San Francisco to London to see if the feeling of tiredness could be shifted to an earlier part of the day. A large percentage of those subjects taking a placebo experienced jet lag after the return to London, but jet lag feelings were nearly absent in those taking melatonin—Anonymous (1986c:34). Noting this same phenomenon, Franks concluded that:

> When interplay of various factors governing the pineal is finally understood, man may be able to adjust his biological rhythm and become nocturnal like an owl for a period of time, or for long-distance international travel. Franks (1988:22)

Melatonin is also a sleep-inducing hormone which depresses mood and alertness—see Begley and Cook (1985:64). This is why darkness is generally conducive to sleep.

A problem with early pineal research was the difficulty in gathering accurate data about the gland and its functions. According to Guyton there were many false starts:

> Literally thousands of attempts have been made to extract hormones from this 'gland' and many such hormones have been claimed and later disclaimed by different research workers. The two most usual hormonal effects postulated have been *growth stimulation and sexual stimulation.* Guyton (1966:1048)

Another problem with drawing conclusions about the pineal gland—Guyton (1966:1048)—is that is becomes partly calcified in about one-third of all middle age adults, a condition which does not seem to have any serious effects on health. Its major effects are evidently most important in youth and adolescence, when growth and stimulation to influence the arrival of puberty are important. In adults the gland may serve as a back-up organ, or some of its functions may be assumed by other glands if it is impaired. Diet or environmental factors may influence the calcification of the pineal gland—see Schmidek (1977).

Melatonin levels decrease in women as they age, particularly in the post-menopausal period—see Wetterberg *et al.* (1970). The pineal gland, or at least its inhibiting effects, are thus less important in older women. Changes in melatonin levels may be responsible for some of the sleep difficulties in menopausal females.

Until recently, the main evidence of the pineal gland's endocrine functions were derived from work with pineal tumor patients. It was found that young male patients with tumors of nonendocrine elements of the pineal (such as connective tissue) exhibited precocious pubertal development. Evidently, this early onset of puberty occurred because the tumor cells also caused the destruction of the pineal endocrine cells, which in turn produced a decrease in antigonadotrophic hormones—Blask (1982). Blask (1982) related further that hypersecretion of pineal antigonadotrophic hormones delays the onset of puberty as well as gonadal development. According to Reiter (1977) melatonin indoleamine, synthesized and secreted by the pineal, is the most likely candidate for the role of pineal antigonadotrophine.

Blask and Nodelman (1979 and 1980), as well as Leaden and Blask (1982) and Leaden (1982), researching the pineal gland's function in regulating conception, found that in rats the pineal gland responds to lighting changes in ways that regulate sexual development, fertility, and the reproductive cycle. The pineal gland secretes hormones that inhibit conception during prolonged darkness. Using artificial pineal gland hormones, reproduction rates have been controlled in experimental animals.

Before the advent of modern artificial lighting, the number of hours humans spent in darkness was much greater. Today, the bright lighting found in almost all homes and offices may be affecting our reproductive cycle. Several workers have suspected that in recent years the onset of sexual maturity at an earlier age, and even the higher rate of multiple births may to some extent be the result of this "light pollution," or exposure to a large amount of light during most of one's waking hours.

Studies completed on "pre-electric" Eskimos support the conclusion that light and the pineal gland are important in reproduction. When it is dark for months at a time, Eskimo women stop producing ova altogether and men become less sexually active. When daylight returns, both the women and the men resume "normal" reproductive cycles.

Some correlation has been shown between the changing of seasons, rising melatonin levels, and peak rates of conception in Eskimos—see Ehrenkranz (1983:18). Peak conception rates occurred in March when melatonin levels were rising, while the lowest conception rates were observed when melatonin levels were very low or very high—summer and winter, respectively.

Circadian Rhythms and Pineal Gland Activity

Regarded by some as a relay station to regulate body phenomena which follow a daily pattern known as a circadian rhythm, the pineal gland may actually regulate what we have in ignorance called the "biological clock." In their first two chapters, Redfern et al. (1985) dealt with melatonin and its important effects on circadian rhythms in general. Its activity in regulating circadian rhythms in birds, as well as temperature cycles in rodents, is well documented—see Scheving et al. (1974) and Leonard et al. (1975). Certain functions such as sleep need to take place within a rhythmic cycle and must be regulated according to both timing and duration. The pineal gland seems to contribute toward, and even control, the sleep cycle. Pineal secretions vary throughout the daily cycle, as noted by Machado et al.:

> In the past 10 years major advances in our knowledge of pineal physiology have been established. Compounds within the pineal body have been identified and their levels measured. Many of them have been shown to have a circadian rhythm that is dependent upon environment lighting mediated through the retina and symphathetic nervous system. Machado et al. (1969:42)

Researchers have identified a marked diurnal fluctuation in the serotinin content of the pineal gland in rats, which are nocturnal animals. The level varies from a mid-day peak at 1:00 p.m. to a night-time trough at 11:00 p.m. This circadian rhythm persists in both blinded rats and those kept in constant darkness—Snyder et al. (1967:206). There is experimental evidence to support the idea that melatonin secretion and melatonin regulate the workings of the "biological clock" in mammals—see Anonymous (1983:802), Romero and Axelrod (1974), Relkin (1976), Brownstein (1977), and Cardinali *et al.* (1972). Normally, the pineal gland secretes melatonin at higher levels at night and lower or undetectable levels in the day—Anonymous (1985a:43). But if mammals are kept in constant darkness the production of melatonin by the pineal gland follows a circadian rhythm with a periodicity of 24 hours, similar to the rhythm followed by serotonin. Mutations of two independently segregating genes can cause the complete absence of melatonin secretion in certain strains of laboratory mice—Anonymous (1986b:26).

Brownstein and Axelrod (1974), as well as Klein and Weller (1970), reported that the rat pineal gland serotomin levels can be altered by the hormone *norepinephrine,* commonly called noradrenaline—see also Klein *et al.* (1973), Deguchi and Axelrod (1973), and Deguchi (1979). In some animals the pineal gland, therefore, does indeed seem to function as a third eye, although it responds to light in a much different way than do human eyes—Eakin (1973). Axelrod concluded that this gland may be the organ of choice for the study of rhythms:

> The pineal gland has become the subject of considerable investigation during the past decade because it provides a productive experimental model for studying circadian rhythms and regulation of [various] organs by nerves. Axelrod (1974: 1341)

Both the retina of the eye and the pineal gland contain melatonin. Similarities such as this between the eye and the pineal gland have prompted some evolutionary biologists to assert that the pineal gland was the precursor of the eye—see J. A. Miller (1985). Because melatonin is present in various tissues in vertebrates, Gern *et al.* (1986) have even tried to deduce which tissue sources are "recent" and which ones are ancient by measurement of melatonin.

Seasonal daylength variations lead to fluctuations in the melatonin secretion by the pineal gland. This produces seasonal changes in appetite and metabolism in both hibernators (like the ground squirrel) and in nonhibernating mammals (like the deer)—see Loudon (1985).

Blask presented an excellent summary of the research on the pineal gland:

> As more data becomes [sic] available, pinealogists will be better able to ascribe a definite functional role to the pineal gland in human reproductive physiology [as well]. Moreover, future clarification of a potential role played by the pineal gland in the menstrual cycle will be enormously useful to clinicians in considering the possibility of anomalous pineal function in the various diagnoses of menstrual abnormalities, infertility and problems associated with menopause. Blask (1982:132-133)

Melatonin is known to have many other functions in humans and animals. It has been shown to influence operant behavior in pigeons—

Schoenfeld (1971). Removal of the pineal gland in rats induces mammary tumors—Anonymous (1985b:153). Far from being vestigial, the pineal gland has been shown to receive nerve signals from the brain and to send messages back to the brain—Anonymous (1986a:122).

The "Nictitating Membrane" in The Human Eye—The Plica Semilunaris

An excellent example of another commonly mislabeled vestigial organ is the so-called remnant of a *nictitating membrane* in the human eye. The following words by Storer and Usinger are an illustration of the misinformation on the plica semilunaris as the human counterpart of the nictitating membrane:

> In the inner angle of the human eye is a whitish membrane representing the transparent nictitating membrane... Storer and Usinger (1977:208)

A nictitating organ is a transparent membrane hinged at the inner side or lower eyelid of many animals, which serves to clean and moisten the eye as it moves across the surface of the eyeball. It has a set of muscles and is considerably different than what has been mislabeled the nictitating membrane in *Homo sapiens*.

In the classic book on the anatomy of the eye, Banks (1981) described the misnamed human nictitating membrane, which is actually the plica semilunaris. Although it is often considered to be homologous with the "third eyelid" of many animals, the plica is not a nictitating membrane. The following detailed description was provided by Wolff (1976:220):

> The plica simulunaris is a narrow crescentic fold of conjunctiva... The pink colour of the plica is due to its vascularity and contrasts with the white of the sclera. In structure it is like that of the rest of the bulbar conjuctiva, but the epithelium, instead of the six layers, consists of eight to ten, and the deepest layer, instead of being cubical, is cylindrical and contains a lobule of fat and some non-striated muscle supplied by the sympathetic [nerve]. Goblet cells are particularly numerous. Wolff (1976:220)

In humans the plica serves as a support and control structure for the eye as well as lubrication and effective eyeball movement. Gardner *et al.* (1975:641) added that "... the fold intercepts foreign bodies on the cornea and passes them to the region of the lacrimal caruncle," the part of the eye closest to the nose.

Bloom and Fawcett (1975) as well as Parker (1928:42) reported that the so-called nictitating membrane in humans is devoid of striated muscles. Without the plica similunaris, comfortable vision would be considerably more difficult.

Another important function of the plica semilunaris is the secretion of mucin, one of the three elements which make up the tear film. For this reason the plica "... is covered with goblet cells, which secrete mucin"—Wolff (1976:221).

The eye has about 50 to 55% rotation. Without the plica semilunaris the eye would have considerably less rotation. Although not needed for survival, the plica does increase the field of vision possible without moving the head, as King (1979) related to Bergman. The plica, supplying such a generous rotation, serves as an example of what is called "overdesign." The plica is almost inevitable, as Wolff (1976:221) reported:

> A still simpler view of the plica semilunaris is that it is an inevitable formation. The conjuctival area here must be generous enough to allow full lateral movement of the eyeball. Thus there is slack to be taken up when the eye looks forwards or medially; hence the fold. No such arrangement exists laterally, for here the fornix is very deep. The absence of a deep medial fornix is a functional necessity to enable the puncta to dip into superficial strips of tear fluid.

To Scadding the semilunar fold is nothing more or less than a:

> ... portion of the conjuctiva at the medial corner of the eye ... [which] ... aids in the cleansing and lubrication of the eyeball ... Scadding (1983:6)

Another function of the plica semilunaris is to collect foreign material that falls on the eyeball surface. To do this, it secretes a sticky mass which collects the foreign material and, in essence, insulates the material for easy removal from the eye without fear of scratching or damaging the eyeball surface. Stibbe heralded the role of the plica in clearing foreign objects from the eye:

> If one goes out in a dust storm, one's eyes rapidly fill with dust, and as rapidly get rid of it. Where does the dust go? It will be found collected together into a little sticky mass at the inner canthus; and that mass is situated on the skin, in the angle internal to the caruncula lachrymalis, in which situation it causes no irritation ... this is brought about by the intervention of the plica semilunaris, which is not so vestigial a structure as the descriptions of it might imply; it is in fact a very respectable fold, with an underlying conjuctival fornix often a quarter of an inch in depth...
>
> If the eye be kept open when there is a foreign body in it, the ball will be seen to be repeatedly turned inwards, in an effort to get the body picked up by the plica and diverted towards the caruncular region. An eyelash, for example, has been observed in a patient's eye; it was carried inwards by the tears and the action of the orbicularis, but slipped under the plica semilunaris; it was brought out from this position by an outward sweep of the eye polishing the deep internal fornix; and after several trials it was finally picked up by the plica, and transferred to the skin at the inner canthus. Stibbe (1927:169-170)

This membrane, although clearly important, has nonetheless often been incorrectly interpreted by evolutionists as a vestigial structure—see Drummond (1903), Parker (1928), Baitsell (1929), Lull (1932), Moody (1953), Duke-Elder and Wybar (1961), and Dodson and Dodson (1976). Many biology and zoology text writers still label it a useless vestige—see Mader (1989) as an example. A. Thomson bluntly concluded:

> ... there is no doubt as to the meaning of this fold which anyone can see in the looking-glass; it is a dwindled relic of the third eyelid which is present in most mammals, as also in birds. A. Thomson (1958:204)

This structure is not a nictitating membrane, and does not serve the function of "nictitating," or blinking, nor is its development or innervation even close to that of animal nictitating membranes—J. King (1979). Although the nictitating membrane and the plica semilunaris have some overlapping functions, the latter is fully functional in humans. It "... does not correspond to the nictitating membrane" in animals as Gardner *et al.* (1975) noted.

The nictitating membrane and the plica are not homologous, according to Weichert (1970:419). The reasons Weichert gave as to why the plica is not homologous with the nictitating membrane revolve around its developmental history, its structure, and its innervation. The latter is by different nerves than the animal nictitating membrane which is innervated by the abducens nerve. Scadding supported this view when he wrote:

> The absence of a nictitating membrane in humans is of no significance to a discussion of the function of the semilunar fold. Scadding (1983:6)

The Eyebrows and Eyelashes Were Once Considered Vestigial

Duke-Elder and Wybar (1961) reported that about 100 or 150 lashes are typical for the upper lid, and about half as many (75) for the lower eyelid. In the upper lid, the lashes are curved outward and then upward. Each lash is a short, stout, cylindrical hair which grows from hair follicles that are similar in structure to those in other parts of the body. Adler and Adler (1965) indicated that each follicle is surrounded by a nerve plexus which has a very low threshold of excitation.

The eyeball surface is a delicate structure needing much protection. The eyebrows and eyelashes reduce the amount of dust that enters our eyes. The eyelashes serve as the first line of defense in the system designed to protect the eyeball. Anything near the eye will almost always touch the eyelashes first, producing both a reflex blink and tears.

The eyebrows also absorb and deflect sweat (which can be a painful eye irritant) from the forehead so it does not flow into the eyes. Moses noted that:

> The eyebrows help to prevent perspiration from flowing or running into the eyes from the forehead. The brows are elevated by the frontalis muscle, depressed by the orbicularis muscle in forced lid closure, and drawn together in the act of frowning by the corrugator supercilii; they are not moved in the ordinary act of blinking. Moses (1975:5)

In many societies the eyebrows serve the very important function of communication. Individuals with small eyebrows and eyelashes are considerably more bothered by sweat, dust and foreign objects in general than are people with larger ones. The structures, although not necessary for survival, certainly contribute to one's comfort, as anyone who has experienced severe eye irritation is aware. The eyebrows are perhaps another example of providential overdesign.

The Ear Muscles

Also commonly labeled vestigial are the muscles which enable some individuals to move their external ear, that is, the pinna or auricle—the portion of the ear which projects from the side of the head. Darwin viewed man's external ear muscles as relics of the *panniculus carnosus* which extended over a large part of the body of the animals he felt were ancestral to humans. This muscle system enables the animal to twitch its skin, scaring insects from the body surface.

The ability of a human to "wiggle" the ears is rare. There are many other anomalies which only certain individuals possess, such as the ability to use one's eye muscle to literally pull the eyeballs approximately half an inch straight out of the orbits. The ear muscle variation is most likely an anomaly which occasionally occurs because of differences between individuals during development. Some researchers have concluded that these muscles are simply one of the thousands of minor characteristics which make each person unique.

People who can wiggle their ears state that the trait is very useful to communicate, to entertain, and even to adjust their glasses without using their hands. Howitt wrote concerning the muscles of the external ear that:

> ... they are nevertheless useful in providing facilities for increased blood supply to the organ, thereby diminishing the danger of freezing ... Muscle is more than simply a contractile organ. It serves as a storehouse for glycogen and is actively concerned in metabolism. Without some musculature in its structure the nutrition of the outer ear might be seriously impaired. Howitt (1947:14-15).

"Darwin's Point" on The Ear

Some workers have suggested that the human flattened outer ear is a vestige of the once useful movable ear such as that commonly found in mammals like rabbits, dogs and cats. The ease with which we can move our head from side to side obviates the need for a mobile ear. The shape of the human outer ear is highly effective in detecting sound. Dewar (1957) argued that if humans had outer ears like dogs, damage to the ear would be considerably more common and serious than it is.

"Darwin's point" is the small projection on the margin of the ear. It is claimed to represent the remains of the tip of the "pointed ear" found on some lower animals—see Kelley (1962). Dewar (1957:168-169) noted that Darwin's point ". . . does not correspond to the tip of the ear of lower animals . . . [and] many breeds of domestic dogs exhibit no trace of this point." There is no relation between the loss of the point and evolution; it seems instead to be part of the tremendous variation found everywhere in the natural world.

The Mamme, Nipples, and Areolae in Human Males

The mammae, nipples, and areolae (the dark circles around the nipples) found in males are primarily a result of embryonic development. If there are two X chromosomes in a zygote, (XX), the basic development pattern is female. If the father contributed a Y chromosome instead of an X, an (XY) zygote results and a male sequence of development normally ensues. Very early in human embryogenesis male and female embryos resemble each other closely. This early common developmental sequence for both males and females can be explained as "design economy"; the same technique is used in many man-made products as we discussed earlier regarding automobiles. During human development certain structures are modified to produce the organs necessary to reproduce and to manifest the physiological differences which facilitate sexual attraction. These traits (called *secondary sexual characteristics*) do not fully develop until adolescence—relatively late in development.

From a design view, there is no need to abolish the general nipple component from males as it might entail major structural changes for which there is no necessity—see Kofahl and Seagraves (1975). Like belly buttons, the male mammae are remnants of a developmental stage.

From the standpoint of function, both the mammae and the belly button clearly do have sexual significance in many cultures—especially our own. In several studies it has been found that the male nipple is subject to sexual stimuli—see Masters and Johnson (1966). It is a sensitive area of the body, and during sexual arousal may become even more so, sometimes painful to the touch. Masters and Johnson found that in both males and females they are a source of sexual stimuli and are thus certainly not vestigial.

In his *Origin of Species* Darwin noted that:

> . . . rudimentary organs sometimes retain their potentiality; this occurs with the mammae of male mammals, which have been known to become well developed and to secrete milk. Darwin (1859:346)

The mammae in human males should be studied more carefully for other possible functions aside from sexual stimulation. The same is true of the clitoris in the female. Its primary function is sexual, obviously an important role, but it, too, may have multiple functions—see Hrdy (1981).

Male Nipples and Embryological Design

The "rudimentary" breast and nipples on every male mammal (including male humans) have other implications for evolutionary theory. Wilder-Smith noted that if mammals were derived ancestrally from reptiles, as macroevolutionists generally assert, mammae on male mammals must be organs that are still developing. This in turn would lead to the bizarre conclusion that someday males will nurse the young:

> . . . mammae must be developing, evolving organs even in male mammals. If these evolving male organs were useless, they could not have developed at all, for they would then have given their owners no advantage in natural selection . . . their usefulness must lie in the past or just possibly in the future. If the latter is the case, then male mammals will, at some future date, happily suckle their young! Or if the function of the male mammae lies in the past, then we must assume that the male suckled the young in the past and that this function was only recently [completely] taken over by the female. Wilder-Smith (1968:105)

Wilder-Smith (1968:105) noted that the female also has some male "vestigial" organs, each of which present the same problems as mammae or nipples on males. An evolutionist could assert that the clitoris of a female is a vestigial penis, for example. Males possess many "female structures" even organs which synthesize female sex hormones, yet they are all still useful for the male. Therefore, an embryological explanation, rather than a vestigial one, is far more tenable for such structures in both males and females. Such an embryological explanation fits fully with the design model of origins.

According to Scadding (1983:6) male structures in females or female structure in males ". . . do not reflect phylogenetic development." Instead, he concluded that these structures arise because of the simple fact that a particular human who is genetically destined to be either male or female develops from an embryo which at the onset is in an ". . . indifferent condition with structures characteristic of both sexes."

In mammals an XY embryo forms testes and acquires male secondary traits while an XX individual begins to manifest femaleness. There is a difference in the rate and timing of gonadal development between the sexes, as Miltwoch (1988) has clearly noted. For example, at the fifth week the human embryo lacks gonads; but if it is an XY individual, it will manifest rapid development of the gonads at 6 weeks, indicating maleness and the early origin of testes. If it is an XX embryo, gonads are smaller and start developing slightly later. They develop at a slower pace, and become ovaries. It is not true that embryos all start out female, as is sometimes assumed. By virtue of its chromosome pattern, each embryo is of one sex or the other; that destiny is fulfilled in response to closely timed chemical signals—see Miltwoch (1988).

Extra Nipples and Mammary Glands in Strange Places

Extra nipples may also occur in female mammals such as bats, whales, and even humans. Awbrey claimed these extra nipples are evidence that bats, whales, and humans:

> ... all share a common ancestor that had multiple mammae along the milk line, and was neither bat, whale, nor human. Awbrey (1983:6)

O'Brien (1983:2) proposed that genetic mutation is superior to the evolutionary view in accounting for supernumerary mammary glands. These extra glands sometimes occur, not only along the milk line where evolutionists claim them to be evidence of vestigiality but also in many other locations such as on the back, arms, or legs.

A uterus may develop in males of the white whale—see Yoblokov (1974:243-244). Pittman (1983:3,9) has proposed that these abnormalities may all be mistakes in the override code, which regulates the expression of the basic code in each created kind, as was explained earlier.

Chiu (1983:1) suggested that evolutionists ought to refrain from explaining any abnormalities as atavistic throwbacks to our supposed evolutionary ancestry. We have already noted that if one is to examine birth abnormalities for phylogeny, one is obligated to take all of them seriously, leading to some bizarre phylogenies—see Section I.

What About The Yolk Sac in Humans?

O'Brien (1983:1-2) described the yolk sac in the human embryo as having been first thought to be a useless remnant, but finally was found to be a functional organ. Sillman challenged O'Brien's remarks as follows:

> Have I missed something in all my years as a biologist of scanning the scientific literature? I can't recall a single reference in the scientific literature to a "proven" function for the yolk sac in the human embryo. In fact, both yolk sac and allantois, two embryonic membranes that are definitely functional in fish, amphibian, reptile and bird embryos, are vestigial in placental mammals. Their appearance in human (or mammal for that matter) embryos certainly does indicate a genetic kinship with the other vertebrates. It doesn't "prove" evolution occurred—but it does quite clearly, along with a host of other structures and functions, point to genetic linkage of all the vertebrates. Which of course is precisely the significance of vestigial organs. Sillman (1985:1)

For another evolutionist who maintained that the yolk sac is a functionless vestige, see Kent (1978:435).

Kaufmann replied to these claims by quoting an authority who showed that the human yolk sac provides blood and sex stem cells:

> The yolk sac appears during the second week, and it is attached to the underside of the embryonic disc. It functions to form blood cells in the early stages of development and gives rise to the cells that later become sex cells. Portions of the yolk sac also enter into the formation of the embryonic digestive tube. Part of the membrane becomes incorporated into the umbilical cord, while the remainder lies in the cavity between the chorion and the amnion near the placenta. Kaufmann (1985:13)

Is The Human Pharynx Badly Designed?

Some evolutionists believe that there are organs which function so poorly that they negate the whole design view of origins and fit only with chance-based macroevolutionism. Although our present topic is specifically vestigial organs rather than the entire argument of dysteleology, it is important to deal with this recurrent evolutionary assertion that there are examples of poor design in the human body. For example, a noted zoologist from a major university corresponded with Howe claiming that the human pharynx is a badly functioning system, explicable only in terms of macroevolution:

> You designate our Creator as being intelligent. What would you think of an architect that would design a building and have the water and gas enter through a common chamber so that whenever one is needed it would be necessary to shut off the flow of the other? Such would be the height of stupidity. But that is what your "intelligent Creator" did when he designed and created man for, as you know, the pharynx serves as a common passageway for air and water. Think of the number of lives that have been lost by food or water getting into or obstructing the air passageway. It certainly would have required very little intelligence for the Creator to have dsigned a more efficient and less dangerous arrangement. Even I could have done so. However, if you trace the evolution of the head and especially the development of the food and respiratory passageways from the fishes up through the amphibians, reptiles and early mammals to man, you will note that the relationship turns out to be a masterpiece of evolutionary achievement enabling aquatic organisms to become adapted to air breathing and thus capable of living on land. Howe (1981a:3)

Readers of the column were asked to respond to this critic and many did so, defending the design of the pharynx. The responses of R. Harris, Kaufmann, Chiu, O'Brien, Mennega, and others are summarized here—see Howe (1981b:2-3).

1. Design is seen in the use of the pharynx as a connection from the air channel to the alimentary canal which helps to dispose of excess moisture in the air channel and debris filtered from the air itself.

2. Having air pressure available in the food channel is useful and at times critical to force inedible objects such as bones, seeds, or cartilage from the mouth. This air pressure also allows expulsion of food stuck at the back of the mouth.
3. The pharynx structure permits mouth and nose to alternate as breathing ports—a feature that is important whenever the nose is plugged or the mouth full of food, or blocked for other reasons.
4. The nostrils can be used when there is need for smaller quantities of filtered air while the oral cavity allows rapid entry of air in larger quantities as occasions demand.
5. Our pharynx connection actually allows both eating and breathing to go on simultaneously with greater efficiency and less body bulk than if we had two separate channels with no connection. If humans had completely separate tube systems for respiration and alimentary tracts, the amount of networking would have been far more complex, providing even greater chance for errors and casualties.
6. Tongue, teeth, palate, and cheeks are necessary for manipulating food but they are also necessary for speech. Intelligent design has the pharynx for food and air tubes in common. Otherwise we would need two separate mouths with many of the same structures, one set for eating and the other for speaking.
7. The olfactory sense in digestion is also part of the respiratory system so that we can carefully "taste" our food; the sense of taste is largely tied to our sense of smell. Otherwise food would be tasteless, as when we have a heavy cold.
8. When food or water enter this wrong tube (trachea) it is not because the system is designed unintelligently, but often it malfunctions because of severe abuse such as eating or drinking too much and too fast, or eating while under the influence of alcohol. People do not usually die because of a poorly designed pharynx but because of its abuse.
9. The zoologist also committed the logical fallacy of "special pleading." He called it ". . . the height of stupidity" for God to execute the human pharynx as a design but suddenly saw the pharynx as a "masterpiece" when performed by evolution. Illogical reasoning, unfortunately, is not uncommon in origins debates.

The pharynx is thus an example of a skillfully designed system.

As Jacob *et al.* concluded, the pharynx is a system in which several functions are efficiently coordinated.

> The pharynx serves as a passage for two systems—the respiratory and digestive. It also assumes an important function in the formation of vowel sounds. Jacob *et al.* (1982:446)

Are Human "Goose Pimples" and Body Hair Vestigial

A topic related to vestigial organs and supposed dysteleology is the assumption that certain organs were useful for one purpose in the past, but are now used for another—Artist (1969). An example, claimed by Merrell, is that the goose pimple system of humans is vestigial to the system still used by animals to fluff out their hair to improve its insulating properties:

> When cold, our mammalian relatives fluff out their fur to increase the insulation of their bodies; we get goose pimples or duck bumps under the same conditions, but the attempt is abortive, for even though the muscles for fluffing the hair are present, the hair itself has virtually no insulating capacity. Merrell (1962:101)

The analogy broke down when researchers discovered that muscle contractions producing goose pimples serve several important functions, such as a warning to the person of body temperature problems. The muscle tension also yields some heat itself. If that increment of heat is not sufficient, a greater muscle tension results in shivering which produces even more heat. Kaufmann provided the following discussion of the function of piloerection in humans:

> At the base of each hair follicle are small muscles called errector pili. When these muscles are stimulated by sympathetic nerve fibers, they pull on the base of the hair follicle causing the hair to become perpendicular to the skin surface. Concomitantly, as the muscle pulls on its attachment to the dermis, it tends to produce a dimple on the skin resulting in the appearance of "goose pimples." In addition, contraction of the muscle squeezes the sebaceous glands forcing oil into the follicle and onto the skin. This total process is called piloerection. If a person is emotionally upset or becomes cold, piloerection usually is an automatic response . . .

> The purpose of piloerection is to protect against heat loss. In most mammals piloerection entraps large quantities of air around the skin surface and provides an increased insulation against the cold environment. Kaufmann (1982:10)

Is Human Body Hair Useless?

As further illustration of the unfounded dysteleological thinking widespread in evolutionary circles, we include the following challenge printed in Howe (1981b:3), in which the zoologist referred to earlier spoke about hair. He asserted that, if there is a Designer, He made a gross error by failing to give human beings a generous coat of hair:

> Why would an Intelligent Creator create the human species without the protective coat of hair which he so generously provided for all other mammals? I have a theory as to why man lost his hair in the process of evolutionary development. I'd like to know, however, what you Creationists have as an explanation. You always know precisely what the Creator had in mind when he created man. Howe (1981b:3)

Among the useful functions of body hair which covers almost all human skin, Kaufmann (1982:10) listed the intensification of touch perception which occurs whenever a hair is moved or bent—see Landau (1981:70). This is a functional advantage of human hair over the hair on many other mammals. R. Harris (1982:10) also noted that the cluster of nerve fibers at the base of each human hair enables it to serve as a nerve amplifier or nerve extender. When the hair is moved, it physically transmits that information to the nerve.

R. Harris supplied an example of how this touch function of human hair operates:

> Take a second to run your pencil across the hairs of your forearm, or even across the very tiny hairs on the back of your finger, without touching your skin, and you'll see what I mean. Touching a small area on the skin also touches hairs which transmit the touch to an additional number of nerve cells. This is useful for everything from detecting a tiny insect to enjoying the gentle caress of someone you love. We sometimes forget that the sense of touch is not confined to the fingertips—it extends over the entire body. R. Harris (1982:10)

Hair also has an important aesthetic function as R. Harris reported:

> Someone might want to discuss the aesthetics of hair—after all, God is not necessarily a compulsive utilitarian. Only the evolutionists think everything must have survival or reproductive value. R. Harris (1982:10)

Human body hair helps to conserve heat, according to R. Harris:

> For protection against the cold, man has thick hair on his head (where 40% of body heat is lost) and fine hairs all over his body. These fine hairs extend the boundary layer (a layer of still air next to any surface—that's why dust doesn't blow off your car when you drive) and reduce the air flow over the skin somewhat. The effect is not the same as fur, or course, and when the cold wind blows, we certainly feel it. But there is a definite benefit. (Have you ever noticed on a cool night you feel slightly warmer when you get goose bumps? Look closely and you'll see those tiny hairs standing erect, increasing the resistance to air flow.) All those little hairs may not seem like much, but it is a fact that many competitive swimmers shave off their body hair to reduce their resistance through the water. R. Harris (1982:10)

R. Harris showed that human hairs even play a role in cooling the body on warm days:

> But man's small hairs are of even more benefit for body cooling than body heating. Their function here is to hold the body's per-

spiration in an even layer, so that it will not just drip off. (The armpits have thick hair because that's the area of heaviest perspiration.) Take a close look at your skin next time you are perspiring freely and you'll see how well the hair shafts utilize the surface tension of water. I think the importance of this function is further evidenced by the fact that men, who with equal exertion perspire much more heavily than women, also generally have much hairier bodies than women. A man produces more heat and requires more cooling. R. Harris (1982:10)

Human hair affords special protection to the scalp as communicated by Kaufmann (1982:10). Eyebrows, eyelashes, nostril hairs, and even hairs in the ear canals also protect various body parts.

Muscle and Bone Variations as Vestigial Organs

Most of the 180-odd vestigial organs listed by Wiedersheim (1895) were small muscles or minor variations in bones, and not glands or discreet organs like the human appendix. We will discuss briefly the claim that some muscles and minor muscular variations are vestigial.

Certain muscles and bone variations are labeled vestigial primarily because they are not present in most people and are not necessary for survival. They are sometimes not even well developed in those persons who possess the variation.

The *palmaris longis,* for example, is a small "cord" running beneath the skin from the front of the forearm to the palm. It is absent in about 10% of the population. But in pronograde monkeys which use their hand for locomotion as well as grasping, this muscle is always present and is fairly well developed. This small muscle can be developed if exercised. Individuals who have it may possess advantages in accomplishing certain physical movements. They may, for example, make better trapeze artists or pianists. Studies of these muscles need to be undertaken to determine whether a clear basis exists for declaring them in any sense vestigial.

Perhaps gifted athletes such as gymnasts and acrobats have certain muscles that some people may not even possess, or perhaps they are able to develop certain muscles to a greater extent. Human abilities appear to be influenced by genetic differences which reflect themselves in body structure. It would be expected that the muscle system likewise would be influenced by heredity. Any individual variations in physical abilities, including movement, strength, and coordination that are superior to what others possess, could relate to hereditary structural differences in muscle and bone construction. These differences do not mean that unused or underdeveloped muscles in a non-athlete are becoming vestigial in humans. The fact that some muscles are not "useful" or highly developed in humans could result partly from our particular Western way of life.

Possession of some muscles that are not regularly used even in an active and aggressive lifestyle better demonstrates "overdesign" or the variation principle than it does vestigiality. It leads to the production of some individuals who are exceptional. These muscle data do not demand the belief that any muscle is becoming vestigial. The assumption that disuse of muscles in modern humans will cause some of them to vanish gradually is based at least partly on the erroneous Lamarckian assumption that disuse causes disappearance.

The fact that some individuals are superior athletes from a young age is evidence that genetic components are clearly important in complex physical activities. DeVries (1980:16-18) maintains that athletic ability depends on variations in numerous aspects of muscle cell structure and physiology. Certain muscles and muscle types must first be present before they can even be developed by proper training. It is a misnomer to call such muscles vestigial.

The argument that some small muscle is vestigial is difficult to refute in that it depends heavily upon interpretation of personal judgments as to the aesthetic value of that particular structure. It is largely agreed that none of the so-called vestigial muscles are in any way detrimental. Indeed, if they are developed in an individual, the possessor of such muscle variants can be clearly seen as having an advantage, even if this is only an aesthetic one.

Wisdom Teeth or Third Molars

Berland and Seyler (1968) noted that the third molars in humans erupt through the gums between the ages of 15 and 22. They are called "wisdom teeth" because by the time they erupt, ". . . the person may be supposed to have acquired some wisdom" (Webster's Dictionary). Actually these teeth begin forming before a child reaches the tenth birthday and sometimes do not erupt until as late as age 23 or older. Impacted wisdom teeth never fully erupt. Problems occur mainly in the lower jaw bone which may not room have for them, although sometimes the dental arch in the upper jaw is not large enough to accommodate new teeth. Berland and Seyler concluded that this crowding:

> . . . causes a disturbance in the wisdom tooth eruption. This molar can be erupting normally and then stop short of piercing the gum. Often, the tooth is lying on its side under the gum, trying in vain to erupt by pushing horizontally on the roots of the second molar. Obviously, the wisdom tooth is misnamed. These foolish teeth even try to erupt backward toward the ear, or—imagine—completely upside down. Berland and Seyler (1968:155)

The main cause of the problem according to J. Harris and Weeks (1973) is that the teeth evolved more slowly than the human jaw. Wisdom teeth are thus commonly used as an example of either a vestigial organ, or evidence that the human jaw is evolving to a smaller size. The major problem with this argument is that it is difficult to comprehend what possible advantage a smaller jaw would have for survival.

Allford, however, concluded that wisdom teeth are often still useful:

> It is generally held that diet and the amount of breast-nursing a child has during infancy have a lot to do with the development of the jaw and teeth. Only some people have impacted wisdom teeth. There are many of us who have good functioning wisdom teeth. Allford (1978:47)

Their purpose, obviously, is to chew food, and those who have them, if they are not impacted, find them very helpful.

J. Harris, professor of dentistry at the University of Michigan, who is both a geneticist and an orthodontist interested in the dentition of ancient man, directed a research project in which limited evidence was found to support the degenerated jaw theory. Harris and Weeks (1973:65f) concluded that modern humans have smaller faces, smaller jaws, and more crowding of the teeth than did our ancestors. The problem with this conclusion, though, is that such changes may in part be caused by diet and environment. J. Harris and Weeks (1973) admitted that poor diet can itself cause slower bone growth in children.

In 1965 J. Harris assembled a staff to study the dentition of the Egyptian mummies. The reason their jaws were larger in the cases he examined could be that these people were part of the upper class; most of the mummies were royalty in their lifetime. Because their diet consisted of hard food, their jaws were more developed than today. A strong jaw is not passed on to one's offspring, but developed in each generation. Most of our modern human food is soft; often the toughest thing our jaw might be called upon to chew is a tough steak or rubbery pizza.

Ignoring above factors, wisdom teeth are explained in terms of discredited Lamarckian evolution. For example, the writer of an article in *Changing Times*—[Anonymous (1966:36)] stated that, "Through succeeding generations [lack of use] . . . has caused [the jaw] to shrink as well as weaken." For the jaw to become smaller by neo-Darwinian evolution, reduced jaw size must have survival advantage, and this hardly seems to be the case.

A smaller jaw would, at best, indicate de-evolution or dysgenetics, not positive natural selection. The limited studies on the pharaohs and their households notwithstanding, evidence exists that the human jaw has not changed in size or shape for more than 6,000, some claim 80,000 years. Montague and Darling rejected the idea that man's jaw is growing smaller:

> Every so often one reads that the orthodontist is prospering as never before because the jaws of man are growing smaller and there is not enough room in them for his teeth to erupt properly, and so they become crowded and malocculded. There is no truth whatsoever in these notions. Man's earliest representatives, the Australopithecines, in several instances exhibited crowded teeth. As our leading authority, Professor Adolph H. Schultz, has stated,

> 'Unequivocal crowding of teeth is quite common among recent wild monkeys and apes. I have never failed to encounter cases with displaced, twisted, or impacted single or several large teeth in collections of primate skulls, and often such manifestation of unmistakable maladjustment in the size of the teeth and the jaws, resulting in crowding, are much more pronounced than in the two or three instances found in the Australopithecines.' Crowded premolars are particularly frequent in all manlike apes and comparatively rare in monkeys. Moderate to very marked irregularities in the alignment of the incisors are suprisingly common among baboons and not at all rare in most other species of recent monkeys as well as apes. Such cases seem to result from insufficiently large bone spaces between the incisors and the canines (eyeteeth). Crowding of permanent teeth is frequently associated with delays in the shedding and replacement of milk teeth. Montague and Darling (1967:73)

In Western society, wisdom teeth have sometimes been a nuisance; if they become impacted they have to be removed. Yet little evidence exists that this problem occurs because the jaw is evolving into a smaller unit. It is also difficult to identify the relationship of wisdom teeth to the jaw because of influences from diet, health, local conditions and racial factors.

Likewise, it must be remembered that in many people the wisdom teeth erupt normally and function in the act of chewing. In dental prosthetics, wisdom teeth may even replace the other missing molars as a mooring point for bridges.

Are Spurs on Snakes Vestigial?

One of the more commonly used examples of vestigial organs in animals are the so-called claws or spurs on the posterior of several types of snakes, such as the boa constrictor, python, anaconda, and others. It is claimed that these structures are vestigial "legs" since they are anatomically located where the hind legs of other reptiles would appear. In most cases, such as the anaconda and the python, they are slightly exposed—see Williams (1970) and Carr (1963).

Griehl espousing the evolutionary philosophy concerning pelvic bones and the spurs in certain snakes wrote that:

> The skeletons of these snakes-still show vestigial pelvic bones and anal spurs that represent the remnants of hind legs. These remnants of legs have, of course, lost all function in locomotion. Griehl (1982:11)

But regarding actual functions for such snake spurs, he added that:

> It is likely that they are used for the male to stimulate the female during copulation. Griehl (1982:11)

The assumption that these snakes had legs in their evolutionary past, but lost them through evolutionary selection, totally lacks fossil evidence. Changes such as the loss of legs would have been expected to be preserved quite well in the fossil record, if they had occurred.

Yet Dewar concluded that these claws are functional in such snakes:

> It is almost certain that these appendages assist in locomotion particularly in the case of large constrictors when climbing trees [their natural habit] or hanging from branches. Dewar (1957:169)

Their usefulness is supported by the way they are attached to the animal's pelvis which seems to make them homologous to the femur—see Dewar (1957). Dewar noted that they are movable by muscles and serve as amazingly strong grabbers. They also ". . . enable the snake to strike a powerful blow with its body, in some cases, even to cut its victim." To achieve these purposes—Dewar (1957:33)—the spurs have ". . . black horny caps on the bone structure—see also Storer and Usinger (1977). Carr (1963:29) likewise indicated that the male uses these movable spurs to scratch (and probably stimulate) the female during courtship.

List (1966:44) cited the earlier work of Essex who theorized that the claws of certain snakes may function during courtship:

> The femur is a bone or calcified cartilage of variable shape and development. . . . [which] . . . bears a cornified clawlike cap which may even extend to the surface by way of a pore in the skin . . . Essex suggested that the claw might be protruded only at the breeding season, functioning in courtship as does the similar spur of some male birds. List (1966:44)

The Hip Bones of the Whale

Other examples given as vestigial organs are the so-called hip bones of whales, located in the region where hip bones are found in other animals. For evolutionary explanations of the whale pelvis as a useless vestigial organ, see Alexander (1975:431), Evans (1987:4-5), Ridgway (1972:7), Watson (1981:33) and Young (1962:667). Scheffer (1976:8) also categorized these whale hips as:

> . . . no more than a pair of slender bones floating in the muscles near the sex organs.

As Evans (1987:4) noted, the pelvic bones of whales are ". . . freely floating in muscle tissue just in front of the anus." Awbrey summarized the evolutionary argument concerning whale hip bones:

> Cetaceans provide still another example [of vestigial organs which favor evolution]. The pelvis is reduced and no longer connects the hind legs to the axial skeleton. The two small bones now function only to support the reproductive and rectal muscles. That fact might fit either design or descent with modification. Awbrey (1983:6)

He qualified the last sentence by writing that since whales sometimes produce abnormal leg bones, only evolutionists can give a parsimonious explanation of reduced hip bones and remnants of leg bones.

Concerning the hip bones of whales, Crapo supported Awbrey in affirming that workers who hold the design view cannot explain the data scientifically:

> ... it is clear that the empirical data fit neatly within an evolutionary argument while posing an unresolved problem for creationists due to lack of fit with their theory. Crapo (1984:6)

Awbrey (1983:6) has grudgingly acknowledged that the two small pubic bones in a whale do function by supporting various organs and muscles and thus may fit within the design model. Researchers have indeed found that these bones support the internal organs and also serve as points of attachment for several muscles—see Williams (1970:33). The same function in the human is served by the coccyx, also claimed for some time to be vestigial, as noted in earlier discussion. Young indicated that the whale pelvis, together with any separate limb bones. "... serve as attachments for the corpora cavernosa of the penis . . ." Young (1962:667)

Watson also recognized this reproductive function of the pelvis in the North Sea beaked whale in which:

> ... the pelvis is present only in males, who seem to use it now to anchor muscles attached to the penis. Watson (1981:33)

Yablokov showed that the pelvis in toothed whales is differentially located in males versus females so that:

> The presence of the pelvic bones makes penis erection possible in the male; they help in the effective contraction of the vagina in the female. Yablokov (1974:234)

Yablokov (1974:235) added that the whale pelvic bones are significant "... because the process of copulation and the normal function of the digestive tract is only made possible by these vestiges."

The Fossil Record of Whales

The acid-test of evolutionary descent is the possible correlation of fossil data with changes that are imagined to have taken place. Awbrey (1983) discussed the fossil record of whales and asserted that it also supports the vestigiality of the pelvic bones because three rather than two pelvic elements are discernible in the fossils. If the fossils manifest a modification from three bones in whales' hips to two (Awbrey cited no evidence), this would not of itself demonstrate that the whale pelvis is now a useless organ.

Various writers have discussed whale origins in light of the fossil record. Their scenario usually starts with extinct creatures found in strata labeled Eocene and placed into a group called the Archeocetes. One of these, named *Basilosaurus*, was at first thought to be a serpent-like reptile, was later reclassified as a "whale-like" mammal—see Evans (1987:2).

It is possible that archeocete types are simply extinct mammals that were unrelated to whales; links between them and fossil whales are nonexistent. Unlike modern toothed whales called the Odontoceti, archeocete fossil forms had teeth that were differentiated into incisors, canines, and molars. There is no fossil connection between the teeth or the pelvic structures of the Archaeocetes and the Odontoceti.

The toothed whales made their debut in rocks called Eocene, about 30 million geological "years" after the Archeocetes became extinct—see Evans (1987:21) and Alexander (1975:434-435). Evans correctly stated that the archeocete fossils of the Eocene were "replaced" by members of four different orders of fossil whales in strata judged to be "Oligocene."

There is thus a lack of clear fossil connections between *Basilosaurus* of the Archeocetes and modern whales, whether toothed (Odontoceti) or baleen. Slijper, as summarized by Gaskin, put this matter bluntly when he noted that:

> Archaeoceti could not be considered as direct ancestors of either modern baleen whales or modern toothed whales . . . it was unlikely that they gave rise to the ancestral forms of either group. The Archaeoceti may be regarded as a less successful independent line which died out perhaps 10 million years ago. Gaskin (1972:3)

The archeocetes may have been members of a separate mammal category, unrelated to modern whales.

When macroevolutionists claim that whale teeth evolved from a "differentiated" condition in fossil whales to an "undifferentiated" teeth in modern Odontoceti, they are to some extent forging a false series involving a serpent-like creature *(Basilosaurus)* on the one hand, and fossil or modern toothed whales on the other. This involves the logical fallacy of *petitio principii*, "begging the question" to be answered, since they are, in effect, comparing unrelated and unlinked life forms. Perhaps this is a satisfying exercise in origins philosophy but it is not based on scientific data.

The claim that there are true polyform teeth in certain fossil Odontoceti [Ridgway (1972:6)] needs more study. Discussing toothed whale fossils in the Squalodontidae of the late Oligocene, Gaskin (1972:3) noted that the teeth were:

> . . . divisible into functional incisors, canines, premolars and molars yet the two latter series were also becoming very numerous and less specialized, a condition found in most modern Odontoceti.

In fossil times there may have been two separate types of Odontoceti—those with polyform teeth like the Squalodontidae and others with no dental differentiation. Only the groups with monoform dentition persisted until today.

The most striking adaption in whales is the presence of the baleen plates in some species, giving them a unique ability to nourish by straining zooplankton from sea water. The origin of the baleen whales is a mystery, as Gaskin casually admitted:

> The first baleen whales, *their origin obscure,* appear in the fossil record for the first time in the Middle Oligocene [Emphasis ours] Gaskin (1972:4)

Evolutionists should likewise be concerned about fossil evidence to support the supposed transition from ancestral land-dwelling mammals to whales. They can now fill this important void only with firm assertions, as in words penned by Gaskin:

> There is near unanimity among specialists that the ancestors of the Cetaceans were also the ancestors of the land mammals known as the Artiodactyla, of which modern representatives are the camels and rhinoceros. Gaskin (1972:5)

But in retrospect macroevolutionists hedge, allowing the perceptive reader to realize that there is virtually no trace of fossil lineage existing between the Artiodactyla and whales, as seen in the following understatement by Gaskin:

> Nevertheless, the fossil record which could confirm the origin of the cetaceans from terrestrial or freshwater mammals *still has many gaps.* [Emphasis ours] Gaskin (1972:5)

Bateman (1985:296) summarized the fossil record accurately by stating that: "The origins of present-day cetaceans are poorly known."

The Leg Bones of Whales

In addition to the small functional hip bones previously described, some whales also have structures that resemble leg bones.

Alexander noted that in some species of whales:

> ... rudiments of a femur and even a tibia are attached to the girdle rudiment. These rudiments are well anterior to the tail flukes. Alexander (1975:431)

Young (1962:667) referred to the whale hind legs as "... bony nodules ... representing limb bones." Watson related that the blue whales:

> ... often have a vestigial pelvis with a tiny piece of the old femur still attached to it. In the Bowhead Whale ... there may also be a tiny tibia. Watson (1981:33)

Awbrey claimed these whale leg bones were atavisms that can be explained only in terms of megaevolutionism. He described them as follows:

> In many cetacean species, an occasional individual also has one or more poorly formed leg bones that form no joint with the pelvis. When present, these bones are arranged in the typical tetrapod order of femur, tibia and tarsus, and metatarsals. The paired protrusions enclosing these leg bones range from tiny bumps to cylindrical structures up to four feet long. Awbrey (1983:6)

There are no fossil data to support Awbrey's belief that these small leg bones indicate the descent of whales from an ancestor that possessed fully formed legs. Byers (1983) has summarized the lack of fossil data for loss of legs in whales:

> The oldest Cetacean fossils are found in Upper Eocene deposits, and in none of these fossils are leg bones better developed than they are in modern specimens. There is nothing aberrant or unusual in these fossils. I have yet to find anything in the fossil record that is surprising or difficult for a creationist to explain. Byers (1983:2)

There are several explanations for whale leg bones and similar abnormalities. Pittman accounts for such abnormal phenomena as problems in the override code package. Whale leg bones may also be mere mutational or developmental abnormalities conveying no phylogenetic information—see "Are Some Babies Born With a Tail"? in Part I.

Teeth in The Whale Fetus

The teeth found in the whale fetus are commonly labeled vestigial. It is assumed that these embryonic "teeth" are unnecessary because they are not present in the adult. Ridgway made the following phylogenetic claim for the teeth of fetal baleen whales:

> That the baleen whales derived from toothed ancestors is suggested not only by paleontological evidence but also by the fact that teeth are still found in . . . [their] . . . embryos. The teeth are absorbed as the fetus develops the whalebone characteristic of this suborder. Ridgway (1972:507)

Awbrey's words (1983:6), further illustrate that certain evolutionists use fetal baleen whale teeth as examples of vestigial organs. He argued that these teeth fit only the macroevolutionary view and that they absolutely falsify the design model. Concerning the design view of origins, he wrote that it is without support.

But if fetal baleen whale teeth have functions, they cannot be rightly called vestigial. Vialleton noted that:

> Even though teeth in the whale do not pierce the gums and function as teeth, they do function and actually play an important role in the formation of the bone of the jaws to which they furnish a *point d'apui* on which the bones mold themselves. Vialleton (1930:164)

Kaufmann elaborated on Vialleton's remarks concerning the function of whale teeth:

> A French scientist Vialleton, author of *L'Origine des Etes vivants*, claims that temporary development of teeth in whales guides the formation of their jaw. The teeth are multiplied and the length of the jaw is patterned after this multiplication. This could apply to the baleen whale; after the jaw is properly formed, the teeth are completely resorbed into the bone structure. Kaufmann (1983:4)

Dewar also eleborated on Vialleton's research. Dewar's discussion is reproduced here at length:

> That Darwin was wrong and Vialleton was right is indicated by the following facts:
>
> (a) To quote Vialleton, ". . . the disposition (of these fetal teeth), their form and their number, different from those of other Cetacea, show that in the whalebone whale, far from being merely the relics of an extinct ancestor, they have an individuality and a causality peculiar to them, since they are multiplied and adapted to the length of the jaw."
>
> (b) It is highly improbable that the ancestors of the toothless whales first acquired a number of additional teeth, then scrapped them all and developed in their place the extraordinary baleen plates that occur in the mouth.
>
> (c) No living or any known Tertiary bird has teeth, but Archeaopteryx and all known Cretaceous birds had well-developed teeth. If, as the evolutionist supposes, modern birds are derived from toothed ancestors, many, if not all, birds should exhibit fetal teeth, as whalebone whales do, but no known bird embryo shows any trace of teeth. The supposed rudimentary teeth that have been described in parrots, are not teeth but papillae, similar to those under the hoof of the horse, which provide horny tissue to make good that worn away. Birds lack embryonic teeth because these are not necessary for the moulding of the very slender jaw.
>
> (d) American ant-eaters lack teeth, and having attenuated bird-like jaws, no teeth appear in the fetus, although embryonic teeth occur in the toothless Edentata of which the jaw is comparatively massive.
>
> (e) The adults of both the known Monotremes, Platypus and Echidna, lack teeth, but while the embryo of the slender-jawed Echidna shows no teeth that of Playtpus does, and these persist for some time.
>
> (f) Confirmation of the correctness of Vialleton's assertion that one of the functions of the developing teeth is to enable the jaw to

> be properly moulded, is afforded by a paper by Dr. John Cameron (*Trans. Roy. Soc. Canada,* Vol. XII (1918)) illustrated by a photograph of a microcephalic idiot of whom the jaws recede like those of an ape, because of the poor development of the teeth. 'In many of these individuals' he writes (p. 179) 'the teeth never develop at all.' The effect of this defective dentition is reflected in the corresponding feeble degree of development of the jaws. . . . The superior and inferior maxilae (jaws) in the early stages of their ossification, it may be recollected, are fragile bony shells enclosing the dental germs. For example, the lower jaw at birth is simply a thin trough of bone enclosing the developing teeth. The cause (of the poorly developed jaws) is a deficiency or actual total failure of development of the dental germs, the effect being that the investing jaws likewise fail to execute their normal growth and evolution. Dewar (1957:171-172).

It would have been more accurate to term these disappearing teeth a unique jaw development system instead of teeth which never erupted from the gums. In several studies using different animals, researchers have found that if the teeth did not develop properly, a feeble jaw resulted.

Dubois developed a critique of the argument that embryonic teeth in baleen whales are evolutionary vestiges. His analysis contains a penetrating review of certain logical fallacies that are inherent within the vestigial organ concept.

> It seems highly unlikely that the baleen whales would have developed the extra teeth only to begin the process of losing them. While there is absolutely no doubt in my mind that the evolutionist could construct an adaptationist scenario to 'explain' such an occurrence, such scenarios are the evolutionary equivalent of the creationist's 'God could have done it that way,' and in terms of actual explanatory value are equally worthless.
>
> Further, that the teeth seem to be 'adapted to the length of the jaw' militates against the assertion of vestigiality since one of the characteristics of vestigial structures is that *they are no longer adaptive* and therefore in the process of being discarded.... I have actually seen one person maintain that *even the degree to which a structure has not yet been lost* is controlled by considerations of adaptive value. I find this incredible. If a structure is useless, how can it be of any adaptive value to maintain it? If it is not useless, then it is not vestigial. . . .
>
> I am left with the suspicion that the question of vestigiality would not even come up except for two factors. First, the evolutionary viewpoint generates certain artifacts—evolutionists must have evolutionary evidence, and 'vestiges' are a phenomenon which

would seem to supply it—but given the number of structures which have been alleged to be vestigial and are so no longer, it may be said that this viewpoint has generated a 'problem' to be 'solved' which is entirely spurious. Second, there seems to be some under-appreciation of the fact that not all structures are directly useful to adults. Dubois (1985:14)

The Horse Splint Bones

The splint bones on a horse, often cited as vestigial, serve two important functions: to strengthen the leg and to allow an attachment for various muscles. Dewar (1957) also noted that they form a groove which cradles the upper part of the suspensory ligament, an elastic brace supporting the fetlock and counteracting the effects of the horse's weight as it walks.

Hayes (1969:44) noted that the horse splint bones are firmly connected together by ligaments. Smythe had this to say about the ligaments:

> The hind surface of the large metacarpal bone is flattened from side to side, and with the small metacarpals, forms a wide groove which houses the suspensory ligament. Smythe (1967:40)

The head of the medial splint bone is the point of insertion of the flexor carpi radialis muscle—see Nickel *et al.* (1986:386). The same author noted that one of the splint bones also serves as the point of insertion of the abductor pollicis longus muscle (p. 388). The fact that these muscles and others find insertion on the so-called "vestigial" splint or metacarpal bones of the horse can be seen in illustrations by Way and Lee (1965:76, 77, 86, 98).

Besides this role of serving as a point for the insertion of important muscles and ligaments, the splint bones help to support carpal bones above:

> The upper ends of these bones aid in the support of the lower row of carpal bones. The inner splint articulates with the second and third carpal bones, the outer splint with the fourth carpal bone. Smythe (1967:40).

Blind Cave Creatures

Certain cave-dwelling fish, salamanders, and invertebrates are blind as adults—see Norman and Greenwood (1975:219-222), Schultz (1948:139-141), Hearald (1961:139-140), Bond (1979:225), Jordan (1925: 419-422), Barker (1964:200), and Smyth (1962:197-203). In his evolutionary review, Loftin discussed cave animals or "troglobites" as creatures which:

> . . . spend the whole or a part of their lives in caves and are incapable of survival in other environments.
>
> . . . Troglobite is a general term which includes such animals as blind cave salamanders, crayfish, insects, isopods, and so forth. . . . Loftin (1988:24)

These blind cave dwelling animals are often cited by evolutionists as support for their loss mutation or negative allometry models.

Loftin asserted that blind cave animals show: ". . . how rapidly an important organ can atrophy and be eliminated by natural selection if it is no longer advantageous. . . ." After admitting that the evidence surrounding many so-called "vestigial" organs is uncertain, Loftin (1988:26) claimed that: "Blind cave animals provide some of the most clear and convincing examples of vestigial organs one can find anywhere."

There are 29 cave-dwelling fish species which are members of 16 different families—Schultz (1948:140). One of these families has five North American cave species, four of which are distributed in the waters of limestone caves in the central United States. The fifth U. S. species is the ricefish, which lives in the streams of the Atlantic Coastal plain and the dark waters of cypress swamps. Although the ricefish has functional eyes, it can find food and survive well without eyes—Hearald (1961:140).

Individuals of the other four cavefish species, when they are young, have functional eyes that:

> . . . become defective and useless in the adult, when they are almost hidden by other tissues. The different parts of the eye are all more or less incomplete, being without function. Jordan (1925:420).

Concerning individuals of these mid-western limestone cave species, Norman and Greenwood (1975:219) reported that, ". . . the eyes are represented in the adults by mere vestiges hidden under the skin. . . ."

The blind goby from the reefs of Southern California lives on the undersides of rocks or in the channels made by crustaceans. Norman and Greenwood (1975:222) wrote that the blind goby's eyes are:

> . . . small and functional in the young but are mere vestiges hidden under the skin in the adult fish.

A similar change from functional eyes to sightless eyes is seen in the grotto or Ozark salamander. The larvae live in above ground springs and brooks where they have functional eyes, while the adults live in caves, wells, and underground streams where they have eyes that, ". . . no longer function, and the lids partly or completely fuse," Barker (1964:200).

This grotto salamander enters caves at the time of its metamorphosis when the

> . . . eyelids close and grow together; the rods, cones, and eye muscles degenerate until the adult can no longer see. Smyth (1962:200).

He also noted that if grotto salamander larvae are kept in light during metamorphosis, they do not lose their eyesight.

The blind salamander of Texas and the olm salamander of the Swiss Alps, which are both blind and unpigmented (white) during adulthood, remain in the larval form as adults—a condition that biologists call "neoteny." Unlike the grotto salamander, these adults have gills and are much larger versions of the larvae. Both larvae and adults of the Texas blind salamander are found only in deep wells and cave waters; at no time in its life history does it enter the light.

While the olm salamander is blind in the caves of the Alps where it develops, the larvae will develop eyes if exposed to red light.

Explanations for Cave Blindness

These troglobites, and many other species not reviewed here, have the propensity for loss of vision and degeneration of their eyes if they live in caves. The genetic packages which control this potential for loss of eyes in adulthood have not yet been discovered, and how these degenerative control mechanisms arose is not understood.

One theory originally proposed to explain the origin of cave blindness was Lamarckism—the disuse hypothesis. Jordan commented on this view and rejected it:

> As to the cause of the loss of eyesight two chief theories exist—the Lamarckian theory of the inheritance in the species of the results of *disuse* in the individual and the *Weissmannian doctrine* that the loss of sight is a result of *panmixia or cessation of selection*. This may be extended to cover reversal of selection, as in the depths of the great caves the fish without eyes would be at some slight advantage. Dr. Eigenmann inclines to the Lamarckian doctrine, but the evidence brought forward fails to convince the present writer that results of individual use or disuse ever become hereditary or that they are ever incorporated in the characters of a species. Jordan (1925:420)

Like Jordan, almost all biologists have rejected Lamarckism for lack of both evidence and a mechanism.

Some evolutionists argue that the whole troglobite phenomenon depends on loss mutations. Already we have noted that the loss mutation model by itself falls short as a means of explaining apparently vestigial organs. As Dewar concluded, the cave habitats simply permit certain mutants to survive, mutants that would be eliminated outside the caves:

> The gene complex believed to control the development of the eyes does not work normally [in these cases]. Should ... mutants [which result in blindness] appear in nature these would soon be wiped out, but, if this happened in a dark cave, there is no apparent reason why blind individuals should not survive to produce offspring. Dewar (1957:173)

In Dewar's view, cave blindness is merely a mutational abnormality which survives in caves because of the lack of selection against it there. Dewar's mutation model allows some variation; the formation of divergent groups (speciation) may have occurred within the limits of the original kinds.

The genetic basis for turning blind in adulthood may involve mutant alleles. In populations of the fish called the Mexican cave characin:

> ... every gradation of eye-form is found, from fully developed and functional eyes to a completely regressed and non-functional aggregate of optic tissue. Different populations of this species show different frequencies of the various eye types. Those living in caves completely isolated from surface drainage are composed almost entirely of fishes with totally regressed 'eyes.' Populations inhabiting less isolated caves show the greatest range of eye degeneration, while fishes living in caves freely connected to a surface river have the highest proportion of individuals with fully developed eyes. Indeed, these eyed forms, although cave-dwelling, are indistinguishable from members of a supposedly distinct genus and species (*Astyanax fasciatus*) wide spread in the rivers of Mexico. Experimental crosses have been made between the two 'genera' and viable fertile offspring resulted. Bond (1979:225)

Bond has provided further detail on Mexican fish showing that lack of eyes and vision in caves results from alleles of loci governing eye development and eye maintenance:

> *Poecilia sphenops,* a livebearer of Mexico, has been noted as having normally sighted forms outside a cave near Tabasco, but with some sightless populations and intergrades inside. Some of the blind individuals are born without sight, while others are secondarily blinded by the growth of circumorbital tissue over the eyes. Cephalic lateralis canals are modified in the cave dwellers, being enlarged and partially open. In addition, those living in the dark depend on tactile stimulation in the courtship behavior rather than the typical visual stimulation generally seen in the species. Bond (1979:225)

Certain human beings possess a recessive autosomal mutation that causes the eyelids to fail to separate, a condition known as cryptophthalmos. Stine showed a picture of an individual affected by this genetic disorder and noted that:

> ... the eyelid and cornea fail to develop on one or both eyes, and the skin of the forehead continues to grow down to the cheeks. Stine (1989:115).

Some evolutionists feel that the tendency toward cave blindness in adulthood results from negative allometry. But blindness is not an automatic result of living in caves, as allometry would predict. The ricefish which have inhabited the dark waters of the Dismal Swamp do not possess the genetic mechanisms for eye loss and blindness in adulthood. Some invertebrate animals such as the spider *Troglophyhantes* are blind in certain caves while in other caves they possess small eyes—see Dewar (1957). In a study of 59 Isopods of the species *Trichoniscus gachassini* living in a cave near Algeria, it was found that:

> ... two near the entrance had small but well-developed eyes, 36 had very degenerative eyes and 21 had no traces of them. Dewar (1957:172).

According to the material compensation principle, one might conclude that eyes of blind cave creatures are reduced because of the increased growth of the body's other organs, whereas in an above-ground habitat the animal's eyes would have developed. Loss of sight above ground would produce for many animals an inability to escape enemies or obtain food. In caves sightless variants are more likely to survive as they have few predators there. While this may be true, the material compensation principle supplies only an observation of what occurs; it does not present a genetic or an origins explanation of the phenomenon of cave blindness.

The words of Schultz typify the uncertainty of evolutionists regarding the origin of cave blindness:

> It is interesting to speculate whether down through the generations the sightless cave dwellers lost their eyes after they had taken up their monotonous and peaceful subterranean lives or, conversely, whether they moved into their sheltered surroundings because they were blind. Still another guess has it that radioactivity in long ages past caused the mutation of the disappearance of organs of sight. Schultz (1948:140)

The degeneration of eyes and loss of sight in some of of these species may be at least partly attributable to environmental influences on the individual as it is developing. It is a well-known fact that if the eyes of newborn puppies are kept artificially closed, beyond the time when they would have normally opened, the visual cortex of such dogs will never develop properly, even after the eyes are finally opened—Meyer (1989). It is possible that the absence of light during a critical phase of ontogeny may cause degeneration of the eyes. A field of experimentation awaits those who would systematically test this idea on organisms that develop in caves or move into caves while they are developing.

It is possible that the Designer originally produced these blind cave fish for their darkened habitats. The design view finds support in that each of the blind fish also has compensatory systems such as ridges of papillae regularly arranged on the head and body—Norman and Greenwood (1975:220). These papillae enable the fish to perceive movements in the water and thus avoid obstacles. It is not clear from any form of evolutionism how life in caves would have produced the genetic basis for these auxiliary sensory systems, nor is it clear how life in darkness would have led to the demise of eyes in adults.

It is possible that at different times during the history of life the Designer has selected certain fish (or other species) and rapidly modified their genetics through non-evolutionary means, equipping them, in this case, for life in newly found cave habitats, a view we discussed earlier.

There is apparently no other mechanism that can account for the presence of blind creatures in specific cave localities; natural selection, material compensation, loss mutation, negative allometry, and Lamarckism are all inadequate. Furthermore, if the cave blindness syndrome had been part of various genomes as they were originally designed, it is not clear how cave-dwelling blind creatures would have survived the global catastrophe or found their way to present locations after the worldwide flood of Noah, as Loftin (1988:26) noted. By combining the ideas of Pittman (1983; 1989) and Lammerts and Howe (1974), we note that perhaps the Designer rapidly added fixup packages to the original genetic codes of cave creatures for adaptive purposes at one or more times long after His original synthesis of the fish kinds.

Since the Designer who modified the life forms later was the One who produced them in the beginning, He is not merely a "God of the gaps" as is sometimes assumed. Loftin wrongly argued that design theorists may not make such an assertion:

> Creationists cannot say that this special act [of producing blindness in cave creatures] took place *after* the Flood, because that would be long after the world was completely finished, according to the opening chapters of Genesis. Loftin (1988:26)

Are There Vestigial Organs in Plants?

The possibility of vestigial organs in plants is one that usually evokes little comment from those who believe that evolutionism is the only acceptable origins model. As Howitt pointed out, that this apparent absence of vestigial organs in botany is a peculiar and puzzling fact:

> Embryonic recapitulation is almost unknown in the plant world although this is where one would naturally expect to find it most clearly demonstrated. A few sporadic resemblances have been noted but they are not impressive. Howitt (1970:22)

Howitt noted that certain botanists suggest that the protonema of a moss harks back to algal ancestry and that in its early stages of growth a fern gametophyte also bears certain resemblances to algae. He added that:

> Instead of a few doubtful cases and isolated instances, however, there should be thousands, if not millions, of clearly defined, unimpeachable in the plant world. . . . if recapitulation had ever taken place . . . Their absence is evidence that recapitulation has never occurred. Howitt (1970:22)

In their continued quest for vestiges, which seemed to be non-existent in plants, certain botanists centered on synergid cells which are located near the egg in the base of the embryo sac of most flowering plant ovules. Evolutionists assumed that the synergids must be remnants of the archegonium—a multicellular vase-like reproductive organ that houses the egg in plants like liverwort, hornwort, and moss that are thought to be "primitive" or "ancestral."

Tempting as the idea of vestigial synergids might have been for evolutionists, Maheshwari (1950) and Battaglia (1951) rejected the concept on anatomical grounds. Still the idea persisted and found its way into well-respected textbooks as evidenced here:

> The synergids and antipodals are short-lived and are believed to be vestiges of functional structures in the ancestors of the flowering plants. Wilson and Loomis (1957:217).

Sinnott and Wilson (1955:477) described synergids as: ". . . perhaps vestiges of an archegonium which has now disappeared."

Foster and Gifford, however, reaffirmed the critical position of Battaglia and put in a few licks of their own:

> . . . an archegonial homology between angiosperms and gymnosperms does not exist. This conclusion serves to emphasize our present ignorance of the phyletic origin and evolutionary history of flowering plants. Foster and Gifford (1959:482)

Without conclusive evidence one way or another, some workers still asserted that the synergids were nothing more or less than vestiges of a larger ancestral archegonium. This seemed to supply some of the vestigial organ data otherwise strangely lacking in the plant world.

Arnett and Braungart (1970:275) portrayed the 8-nucleate embryo sac of flowering plants as a structure parallel to the gametophyte of the fern. When discussing this same structure, Fuller *et al.* (1972:458) wrote that:

> Usually only the two polar nuclei and the egg cell are involved in reproduction. The remaining cells are interpreted as vestigial structures or 'evolutionary holdovers.'

In the absence of data bearing on possible functions, curious speculation about vestigial organs thus arose. From this speculation evolutionary ideology became a type of "antiknowledge" by which synergids were relegated to a "nothing more than" status until someone scientifically studied the function of synergids. Vestigial organ logic thus served to work against the discovery of physiological functions for synergids.

A Guidance Chemical for Pollen Tubes

It has been discovered that a "period acid-Schiff's substance" (PAS substance) is produced in the lower end of the embryo sac of *Paspalum orbiculara*, a type of joint-grass. Chao (1971) supplied strong support that PAS substance may be produced in the synergids. PAS substance apparently guides the growing pollen tube, containing the sperm, on its path from the stigma to the ovule where the egg resides:

> Thus the function of this substance may be considered to be both mechanical and chemotropic. This substance provides a way of

least resistance for the pollen tube and guides it toward its ultimate destination. Chao (1971:652)

While Chao did not confirm that PAS substance is definitely chemotropic, he did show by its physical characteristics that the PAS substance is quite similar to a chemotropic factor that had been discovered previously in the ovules of lilies. He concluded that the PAS substance was being synthesized by synergid cells as they underwent degeneration. Botanists had wondered why synergids disintegrate at an advanced stage in embryo sac development.

Thought at first by evolutionists to be a vestige of an ancestral archegonium, the synergids of flowering plant ovules are instead the likely centers for synthesis of a guidance chemical (pheromone) involved in flowering plant reproduction. These botanical data certainly fit the belief that each group of cells in plants was designed to fulfill specific functions.

In Conclusion

In conclusion, the evidence supports Howitt who wrote:

> Wiedersheim . . . listed 180 [vestigial organs] in the human body. But with the increase of knowledge it has been found that every one of them has an important function. There are, indeed, no vestigial remains in nature . . . Howitt (1972:51)

We have answered Moody's challenge (p. 40) fully:

> It is difficult to explain the presence of useless vestiges . . . by special creation without imputing to the Creator some lack of skill in planning or construction. Accordingly, opponents of the idea of evolution commonly maintain that organs like the appendix are not useless at all, that they have functions which we have never been able to discover. Clearly the burden of proof lies with the affirmative in the matter of proving the usefulness of vestiges for which no functions have ever been discovered. Many readers can testify from personal experience that the advantages of having the organ removed far outweigh the disadvantages.

Moody (1953:42) was wrong in writing that "Occasional mistakes may be made in labeling small organs as rudimentary, but it seems entirely unlikely that the percentage of error is high." There appear to be no useless vestigial organs in humans. Every structure seems to be functional at some point in the human lifespan, disproving Parker's statement that:

> Man, both in his embryonic and his adult state, possesses an abundance of vestigial organs. In fact, students of this subject who have tabulated these parts have attributed to the human being almost a hundred such organs, and though some of these may on further investigation prove not to be true examples of vestigial parts, most of them certainly fall into this class, so that man may be said to be rich in organs of this kind. Parker (1928:46)

The scientific evidence in this review allows us to view the human body and each animal or plant as coordinated units in which the various organs are highly interdependent and functional. Furthermore, almost every organ has multiple functions. Although some organs are more important than others during certain stages of development, all serve an important function at some time during the organism's life. Disease, improper living, and poor nutrition each have taken their toll so that certain structures may appear less useful than they were designed to be. Hereditary defects are also important in decreasing the utility of various organs in individuals.

The concept of vestigial organs has been a side-track which has at times resulted in rather negative consequences. Instead of proclaiming an organ or structure useless, we should ask, "What function or functions does it have?" This positive approach is now gaining sway in biological theory and philosophy, as Scadding (1981: 5-6) has concluded that ". . . vestigial organs provide no evidence for evolutionary theory."

This abandonment of the whole vestigial organ idea should permeate the field of biological science. As Meyer stressed relative to Scadding's conclusions:

> It is not often that one finds an evolutionist totally rejecting one of the historical 'pillars of evolution.' Still less common is to find an evolutionary journal willing to print such 'heresy.' Because of this [Scadding's] paper . . . provides a very important and helpful connecting link in the self-correcting servomechanism of open and free discussion of all sides of controversial issues. . . .
>
> It is to be hoped that this devastating critique of the vestigial organ argument will be widely read. The paper will be especially valuable to teachers and students of the life sciences who regularly encounter dogmatic presentation of this viewpoint. Meyer (1982:190)

But even if all "vestigial" organs are shown in fact to be functional, we will not necessarily disprove evolution in the minds of some because evolution is a closed system; within it, virtually any exception, anomaly, or problem can to some degree be "explained." Even though the coccyx is an important part of the skeletal structure, serving as an attachment for various muscles, it is similar to the base of the tail in animals that have tails. Those who prefer to believe that the cocyx is the remnant of a tail can continue to do so even though it has important functions in humans.

Since virtually all of the so-called vestigial organs are shown to have functions, macroevolutionists can no longer credibly claim that evolutionism is the only origins model that will accommodate these scientific data. Individuals who are not fully indoctrinated with evolutionary philosophy will be able to see that all body organs function harmoniously. Dispelling the concept of vestigial organs allows the Creator's work in biology to be viewed scientifically as neither evolutionary, defective, nor capricious, but as evidence for His handiwork and design.

REFERENCES

Adler, Irving and Ruth Adler. Evolution. 1965. John Day and Co., New York.

Alexander, Barbara, Allen Dowd and Albert Woflson. 1970. Effect of continuous light and darkness on hydroxyindole-o-metyltransferase and 5-hydroxytroptophan decarboxylase activities in the Japanese quail. *Endocrinology.* 86:1441-1443.

Alexander, R. McNeill. 1975. The chordates. Cambridge University Press. Cambridge, England.

Allford, Dorothy. 1978. Instant creation—not evolution. Stein and Day, New York.

Andrews, Roy Chapman. 1946. Meet your ancestors. The Viking Press, New York.

Anonymous. 1966. Why oh why are there wisdom teeth? *Changing Times* June, p. 36.

Anonymous. 1983. Melatonin drives the internal clock. *New Scientist* 97 (1350):802.

Anonymous. 1985a. How daylight influences the pineal gland. *New Scientist* 107(1466):43.

Anonymous. 1985b. Breast cancer and sense of smell. *Science News* 128 (10):153.

Anonymous. 1986a. Pineal gland speaks to brain. *Science News* 129(8):122.

Anonymous. 1986b. Laboratory mice lose their reproductive rhythm. *New Scientist* 109(1498):26.

Anonymous. 1986c. Time is running out for jet lag. *New Scientist* 110 (1508):34.

Anthony, Catherine Parker. 1963. Textbook of anatomy and physiology, Sixth edition. C. V. Mosby, St. Louis.

Archer, O. K., B. W. Papermaster and R. W. Good. 1964a. Thymectomy in rabbit and mouse: consideration of time of lymphoid peripheralisation In: The thymus in immunobiology. Edited by R. A. Good and A. E. Gabrielsen. Hoeber-Hoeber, New York.

Archer, O. K., D. E. R. Sunderland and R. A. Good. 1964b. The developmental biology of lymphoid tissue in the rabbit. *Laboratory Investigations* 13:259.

Arendt, Josephine. 1985. The pineal: a gland that measures time? *New Scientist* 107(1466):36-38.

Arnett, R. H. and D. C. Braungart. 1970. An introduction to plant biology, Third edition. C. V. Mosby, St. Louis.

Artist, Russell. 1969. The concept of homology. *Creation Research Society Quarterly* 6:55-64, 66.

Asimov, Issac. 1963. The human body: its structure and operation. Houghton Mifflin, Boston.

Awbrey, Frank T. 1983. Giving evolutionists some space—vestigial organs demand evolution. Edited by G. Howe. *Origins Research* 6(1):6.

Axelrod, Julius. 1974. The penial gland: a neurochemical transducer. *Science.* 184:1341-1348.

Baitsell, George (Editor). 1929. The evolution of earth and man. Yale University Press, New Haven, CT.

Banks, William J. 1981. Applied veterinary histology. Williams and Wilkins, Baltimore.

Barker, Will. 1964. Familiar amphibians and reptiles of America. Harper and Row, New York.

Bartel, Max. 1984. Die geschwanzten menschen. *Archiv Anthropologie* 15(45): 45-106.

Bateman, Graham (Editor). 1985. The encyclopedia of aquatic life. Facts on File Publications. New York.

Battaglia, E. 1951. The male and female gametophytes of angiosperms—an interpretation. *Phytomorphology* 1:87-116.

Begley, Sharon and William Cook. 1985. The SAD days of winter. *Newsweek* 155(2):64. January 14.

Bergman, Jerry. 1992. The biological theory of atavism: a history and evaluation. *Creation Research Society Quarterly* 29:33-44.

Berland, Theodore and Alfred E. Seyler. 1968. Your child's teeth. Meredith Press, New York.

Bierman, Howard R. 1968. Human appendix and neoplasia. *Cancer* 21(1): 109-118.

Birdsell, J. B. 1972. Human evolution: an introduction to the new physical anthropology. Rand McNally. Chicago.

Blask, David and Jacqueline L. Nodelman. 1979. Antigondotrophic and prolactin-inhibitory effects of melatonin in anesmic male rats. *Neurendocrinology*. 29:406-412.

Blask, David, Jacqueline L. Nodelman, Christopher Leadem and Bruce Richardson. 1980. Influence of exogenously administered melatonin on the reproductive system and prolactin levels in underfed male rats. *Biology of Reproduction* 22:507-512.

Blask, David. 1982. Potential role of the pineal gland in the human menstrual cycle. Chapter 9 in Changing perspectives on menopause. Edited by A. M. Voda. University of Texas Press, Austin.

Bloom, William and Don Wayne Fawcett. 1975. A textbook of histology. Saunders, Philadelphia.

Bolande, Robert P. 1969. Ritualistic surgery—circumcision and tonsillectomy. *New England Journal of Medicine* March 13, pp. 591-595.

Bond, Carl E. 1979. Biology of fishes. W. B. Saunders, Philadelphia.

Bowden, John. 1973. Creation or evolution? The Rationalists Association Chippendale, New South Wales, Australia.

Boyden, A. 1947. Homology and analogy: a critical review of the meanings and implications of these concepts in biology. *American Midland Naturalist* 37: 648-669.

Brownstein, Michael and Julius Axelrod. 1974. Pineal gland: 24-hour rhythm in norepinephrone turnover. *Science* 184:163-165.

Brownstein, Michael. 1977. Mini-review: the pineal gland. *Life Sciences* 16:1363-1374.

Brum, G. L. D. and Larry K. McKane. 1989. Biology: exploring life. John Wiley, New York.

Byers, R. C. 1983. In: Do vestigial organs demand evolution? Edited by G. Howe. *Origins Research* 6(2):2.

Cardinali, Daniele, Frances Larin and Richard J. Wortman. 1972. Control of the rat pineal gland by light spectra. *Proceedings of the National Academy of Science* 69:2003-2005.

Carr, Archie. 1963. The reptiles. Time Inc. New York.

Cartmill, Matt, William L. Hylander and James Shafland. 1987. Human structure. Harvard University Press, Cambridge, MA.

Chase, Francine. 1957. A visit to the hospital. Grosset and Dunlap, New York.

Chao, Chuan-Ying. 1971. A periodic acid-schiff's substance related to the directional pollen tube into embryo in *Paspalum* ovules. *American Journal of Botany* 58:649-654.

Chiu, Christopher. 1983. Do vestigial organs demand evolution? Edited by G. Howe. *Origins Research* 6(2):1.

Clark, Wilfred E. LeGros. 1934. Early forerunners of man. Balliere, Tindall and Cox, London.

Clayton, John. 1983. Vestigial organs continue to diminish. *Focus on Truth* 6(1): 9-23.

Compton's Picture Encyclopedia. 1956. Volume II. Compton's Co., Chicago.

Cooper, M. D., D. Raymond, A. Peterson, H. A. South and R. A. Good. 1966. The function of the thymus system and bursa system in chicken. *Journal of Experimental Medicine* 123:75-102.

Crapo, Richley. 1984. Vestigial organs revisited. Edited by G. Howe. *Origins Research* 7(2):1 ff.

Crapo, Richley. 1985. Are the vanishing teeth of fetal baleen whales useless? Edited by G. Howe. *Origins Research* 8(1):1ff.

Culp, G. Richard. 1975. Remember thy Creator. Baker Book House, Grand Rapids, MI.

Darwin, Charles. 1859. The origin of species. Modern Library, New York.

Darwin, Charles. 1874. The descent of man and selection in relation to sex. Modern Library, New York.

Davidheiser, Bolton. 1966. Evidences and mechanisms of evolution. *Bible Science Newsletter* 4(1):1.

Davidheiser, Bolton. 1969. Evolution and Christian faith. Presbyterian and Reformed Publishing, Nutley, NJ

Davis, Watson. 1960. Appendix may help save cancer victims. *Science Newsletter* 78(5):66.

Dawkins, Richard. 1986. The blind watchmaker. Longmans Group, Harlow Essex, U.K. Creationist reviews of Dawkins' book have appeared in *Origins Research* 1988 11(2):10ff and in *Creation Research Society Quarterly* 1988 24:201-204.

Dawson, Mary. 1978. The role of the human appendix in immunity to infections. *Journal of Pharmacy and Pharmacology* 30(12):90.

DeBeer, Gavin. 1971. Homology, an unsolved problem. Oxford University Press, Ely House, London.

Defendi, Vittorio and Donald Metcalf (Editors). 1964. The thymus. Wistar Institute Press, Philadelphia.

Deguchi, Takeo and Julius Axelrod. 1973. Supersensitivity and subsensitivity of the B-adrenegic receptor in pineal gland regulated by catecholamine transmitter. *Proceedings of The National Academy of Science* 70:2411-2414.

Deguchi, Takeo. 1979. Characteristics of serotonin-acetyl coenzyme A N-acetyltransferase in pineal gland of rat. *Journal of Neurochemistry* 24:1082-1085.

Denton, Michael. 1986. Evolution: theory in crisis. Adler and Adler, Bethesda, MD.

DeVries, Herbert. 1980. Physiology of exercise for physical education and athletics. W. C. Brown, Dubuque, IA.

Dewar, Douglas. 1946. Science and pseudo-science re vestiges and fossils. *Evolution Protest Movement* 13:8.

Dewar, Douglas. 1947. Do vestigial organs exist? *Evolution Protest Movement* 14:8.

Dewar, Douglas. 1957. The transformist illusion. Dehoff Publications, Murfreesboro, TN.

Dodson, Edward and Peter Dodson. 1976. Evolution: process and product. Second edition. Van Nostrand, New York.

Dodson, Edward and Peter Dodson. 1985. Evolution process and product. Third edition. Prindle, Weber and Schmidt. Boston.

Drummond, Henry. 1903. The ascent of man. James Potts and Co., New York.

Dubois, Paul. 1985. Further comments on baleen fetal teeth and functions for yolk sacs. *Origins Research* 8(2):13-14.

Duke-Elder, Steward and Kenneth Wybar. 1961. The anatomy of the visual system. Vol. II. C. V. Mosby, St. Louis.

Eakin, Richard. 1973. The third eye. University of California Press, Berkeley.

Eden, Alvin. 1977. When should tonsils and adenoids be removed? *Family Weekly* September 25, p. 24.

Ehrenkranz, Joel R. L. 1983. A gland for all seasons. *Natural History* 92(6):18.

Eimer, G. H. T. 1901. Die entsetehung der arten. 3 Vols. Leipzig, Germany.

Elves, Michael W. 1972. The lymphocytes. Year Book Medical Publishers, Chicago.

Erzin, Calvin, John Godden, Robert Volpi and Richard Wilson. 1973. Systematic endocrinology. Harper and Row. New York.

Evans, Peter G. H. 1987. The natural history of whales and dolphins. Facts on File Publications, New York.

Fisher, R. A. 1958. The genetical theory of natural selection. Dover, New York.

Foster, A. S. and E. M. Gifford, Jr. 1959. Comparative morphology of vascular plants. W. H. Freeman, San Francisco.

Franks, Robert H. 1988. Vestigial organs. *Ex Nihilo* 10(2):22-24.

Fuller, H. J., Z. B. Carothers, W. W. Payne and M. K. Balbach. 1972. The plant world. Fifth edition. Holt Rinehart and Winston, New York.

Gaines, William. 1964. Three ring mad. New American Library, New York.

Galton, Lawrence. 1976. All those tonsil operations: useless? dangerous? *Parade*. May 2, pp. 26ff.

Gardner, Ernest, Donald Gray and Ronan O'Rahilly. 1975. Anatomy: a regional study of human structure. Fourth edition. W. B. Saunders, Philadelphia.

Gaskin, D. E. 1972. Whales, dolphins and seals. St. Martin's Press, New York.

Geoffroy St. Hillaire, E. 1822. Philosophie anatomique. Paris.

Gern, William A., David Duvall and Jeanne M. Nervina. 1986. Melatonin: a discussion of its evolution and actions in vertebrates. *American Zoologist* 26:985-996.

Gish, Duane T. 1983. Evolution and the human tail. *Impact Acts and Facts* (March).

Glick, B., T. S. Chan and R. G. Jaap. 1956. Bursa of Fabricus and antibody production. *Poultry Science* 35:79.

Good, Robert. 1973. Immunodeficiency in developmental perspective. Academic Press, New York.

Goodrich, Edwin S. 1924. Living organisms: an account of their origin and evolution. The Claredon Press, Oxford, England.

Gould, Stephen J. 1982. Fascinating tails. *Discover* 3(9):40-41.
Grant, Verne. 1977. Organismic evolution. W. H. Freeman, San Francisco.
Gray, Henry. 1966. Gray's anatomy. Lea Febiger, Philadelphia.
Gray, Henry. 1985. Anatomy of the human body. Lea Febiger, Philadelphia.
Greiner, A. C. and S. C. Chan. 1978. Melatonin content of the human pineal gland. *Science* 199:83-84.
Greisheimer, Esther and Mary Wideman. 1972. Physiology and anatomy. Ninth edition. J. B. Lipincott, Philadelphia.
Griehl, Klaus. 1982. Snakes, giant snakes and non-venomous snakes in the terrarium. Barrons' Educational Series, New York.
Gross, Martin L. 1966. The doctors. Random House, New York.
Guyton, Arthur. 1966. Textbook of medical physiology. W. B. Saunders, Phildelphia.
Hackenbruch, P. 1888. Experimentelle und histologishe Untersuchungen uber die Kompensation—Hypertrophie der Testikel. (Dissertation). Bonn, Germany.
Haeckel, Ernst. 1876. The history of creation. H. S. King, London.
Hall, Simpson. 1941. Diseases of the nose, throat and ear. E. and S. Livingston, New York.
Hanaoka, M., K. Nomoto and Byron H. Waksman. 1970. Appendix and gamma-M-antibody formation: I. immune response and tolerance to gamma globulin in irradiated, appendix-shielded rabbits. *The Journal of Immunology* 104:616-625.
Harris, James and Kent Weeks. 1973. X-raying the pharaohs. Charles Scribner's Sons, New York.
Harris, Robert. 1982. In: How can creationists explain human hair? Edited by G. Howe. *Origins Research* 5(2):10.
Hartl, Daniel. 1980. Principles of population genetics. Sinover Association, Boston.
Haupt, Arthur. 1940. Fundamentals in biology. McGraw-Hill, New York.
Hayes, M. Horace. 1969. Points of the horse. Arco, New York.
Hearald, Earl S. 1961. Living fishes of the world. Doubleday, Garden City, New York.
Hedtke, Randall. 1983. Secret of the sixth edition. Vantage Press, New York.
Heinze, Thomas. 1973. Creation vs. evolution handbook. Baker Book House, Grand Rapids, MI.
Heller, Alfred. 1972. Neuronal control of brain serotonin, *Federation Proceedings* 31:81-90.
Herskowitz, M. S. 1964. The mechanistic distortion in treatments of infants and children. *Journal of American College of Neuropsychology* 3:13-18.
Howe, George F. 1971. Homology, analogy and creative components in plants. In: Scientific studies in special creation. Edited by W. E. Lammerts. Creation Research Society Books, Kansas City, MO
Howe, George F. and P. Williams Davis. 1971. Natural selection re-examined. *Creation Research Society Quarterly* 8:30-43.
Howe, George F. and Walter E. Lammerts. 1980. Biogeography from a creationist perspective: II. The origin and distribution of cultivated plants. *Creation Research Society Quarterly* 17:4-18.
Howe, George F. 1981a. Correspondence series. *Origins Research* 4(1):3.
Howe, George F. 1981b. Correspondence series. *Origins Research* 4(2):2-3.

Howitt, John R. 1947. Evolution: science falsely so-called. Ninth edition. International Christian Crusade, Toronto, Canada.

Howitt, John R. 1970. Evolution: science falsely so-called. Eighteenth edition. International Christian Crusade, Toronto, Canada.

Howitt, John R. 1972. Some observations on the science of nutrition in the light of the scriptures. *Creation Research Society Quarterly* 9:51-53.

Hrdy, Sarah. 1981. The woman that never evolved. Harvard University Press, Cambridge, MA.

Jacob, Stanley, Clarice Francone and Walter Lossow. 1978. Structure and function in man. Fourth Edition. W. B. Saunders, Philadelphia.

Jacob, Stanley, Clarice Francone and Walter Lossow. 1982. Structure and function in man. W. B. Saunders, Phildelphia.

Jacquard, Albert. 1970. The genetic structure of populations. Springer-Verlag, New York.

Jensen, D. 1976. Principles of physiology. Appelton Century Crofts, New York.

Jordan, David Starr and Vernon Lyman Kellogg. 1908. Evolution and animal life. B. Appleton, New York.

Jordan, David Starr. 1925. Fishes. D. Appleton, New York.

Katz, Dolores. 1972. Tonsillectomy: boom or boondoggle? *The Detroit Free Press*, April 13, p. 1-C.

Kaufmann, David. 1982. How can creationists explain human hair. *Origins Research* 5(2):10.

Kaufmann, David. 1983. When is a vestige not a vestige? *Origins Research* 6(2):4.

Kaufmann, David. 1985. Further comments on baleen fetal teeth and functions for yolk sacs. *Origins Research* 8(2):13-14.

Kawanishi, H. 1987. Immunocompetence of normal appendiceal lymphoid cells: *in vitro* studies. *Immunology* 60(1):19-28.

Keith, Arthur. 1936. The human body, Thorton-Butterworth. London.

Kelly, Peter. 1962. Evolution and its implications. Hawthorne Books, New York.

Kent, George C. 1978. Comparative anatomy of the vertebrates. C. V. Mosby, St. Louis.

Key, Thomas H. 1959. The influence of Darwin on biology. In: Evolution and Christian thought today. (Russell Mixter, editor) Eerdman's, Grand Rapids, MI.

Kimball, J. W. 1974. Biology. Third edition. Addison-Wesley, Reading, MA.

King, Barry and Mary Jane Showers. 1964. Human anatomy and physiology. W. B. Saunders, Philadelphia.

King, John. 1979. Personal communication. October 18. Dr. King is a professor of ophthalmology at The Ohio State School of Medicine and an authority on the eye.

Kinsey, Alfred. 1920. An introduction to biology. J. B. Lipincott, Philadelphia.

Klein, David C. and Joan L. Weller. 1970. Indole metabolism in the pineal gland: A circadian rhythm, in N-acetyltransferase. *Science* 169:1093.

Klein, David C., A. Yuweller, John Weller and Selma Plotkin. 1973. Postsynaptic adrenergic-cyclic AMP control of the serotonin content of cultured rat pineal glands. *Journal of Neurochemistry* 21:1261-1271.

Klotz, John. 1970. Genes, Genesis and evolution. Concordia Publishing House, St. Louis.

Kluge, Arnold (Editor). 1977. Chordate structure and function. Second edition. Macmillan, New York.

Kochs, W. 1897. Versuche uber die regeneration von organen bie amphibien. *Archiv Mikroskopic Anatomie* 49:441-461.

Kofahl, Robert and Kelly Segraves. 1975. The creation explanation. Harold Shaw Publishers, Wheaton, IL.

Kretchmer, Robert, Say Burhan, David Brown and Fred Rosen. 1968. Congenital aphasia of the thymus gland. *The New England Journal of Medicine* 279:24.

Krumbiegel, J. 1931. Das segenannte kompensatoinsgesetz goethes betr korrelation von kopfwaffen under oberzahnen. *Z. Savgetierkde* 6:198-202.

Lammerts, Walter E. and George F. Howe. 1974. Plant succession studies in relation to micro-evolution. *Creation Research Society Quarterly* 10:208-228.

Landau, B. R. 1981. Essential human anatomy and physiology. Scott Foresman, Glenview, IL.

Lankford, T. Randall. 1976. Integrated science for health students. Reston Publishing, Reston, VA.

Leaden, Christopher and David Blask. 1982. Pineal gland inhibition of prolactin cell activity is independent of gonadal regression, *Neuroendocrinology* 35: 133-138.

Leaden, Christopher. 1982. A comparative study of the effects of the pineal gland on prolactin synthesis storage and release in male and female blind anosmic rats. *Biology of Reproduction* 26:413-421.

Ledley, F. D. 1982. Evolution of the human tail. *The New England Journal of Medicine* 306:1212-1215.

LeGross Clark, Wilfred. 1934. Early forerunners of man. Balliere, Tindall and Cox, London.

Leonard, B. E., V. Neuhoff and Sally R. Tonge. 1975. The effect of the chronic administration of D-amphetamine upon circadian changes in amino acids in the pineal and pituitary glands of the rat. *Neuroscience Research* 1:83-92.

Levey, Ralphael. 1964. The thymus hormones. *Scientific American* 211(1):66-77.

Lipton, Samuel. 1962. On the psychology of childhood tonsillectomy. In: The psychoanalysis study of the child. International Universities Press, New York.

List, James Carl. 1966. Comparative osteology of the snake families. Typhlopidae and Leptotyphlopidae. The University of Illinois Press, Champaign.

Lockhart, R. D., G. F. Hamilton and F. W. Fyfe. 1959. Anatomy of the human body. J. B. Lippincott, Philadelphia.

Loftin, Robert W. 1988. Caves and evolution. *Creation/Evolution* 23:21-28.

Loudon, Andrew. 1985. A gland for all seasons. *New Scientist* 107(1466): 40-43.

Luckey, T. D. (Editor). 1973. Thymic hormones. University Park Press, Baltimore.

Lull, Richard Sawnn. 1932. Organic evolution. Macmillan. New York.

Machado, Conceicao, Laurence Wragg and Angelo Machado. 1969. Circadian rhythm of serotonin in the pineal body of immunosympathectomixed immature rats. *Science* 164:442-443.

Mader, Sylvia. 1988. Inquiry into life. W. C. Brown, Dubuque, IA.

Maheshwari, P. 1950. An introduction to the embryology of the angiosperms. McGraw-Hill, New York.

Maisel, Albert. 1966. The useless glands that guard our health. *Reader's Digest*, November, pp. 229-235.

Marti-Ibanez (Editor). 1970. Tuber of life. *M. D. Magazine* 14:237-247.

Masters, William, and Virginia Johnson. 1966. Human sexual response. Little Brown, Boston.

Merrell, David. 1962. Evolution and genetics. Holt, Rinehart and Winston, New York.

Meyer, John. 1982. Vestigial organs (if they exist at all) prove nothing. *Creation Research Society Quarterly* 19:190-191.

Meyer, John. 1989. Personal conversation with Howe.

Miller, J. F. 1961. Immunological function of thymus. *Lancet* 2748:247-248.

Miller, Julie Ann. 1985. Eye to (third) eye. *Science News* 128(19):298-299.

Miltwoch, Ursula. 1988. The race to be male. *New Scientist* 120(1635):30-42.

Mixter, Russell (Editor). 1966. Evolution and Christian thought today. Eerdmans, Grand Rapids, MI.

Montague, Ashley and Edward Darling. 1967. The prevalence of nonsense. Harper and Row, New York.

Moody, Paul. 1953. Introduction to evolution, Third edition. Harper and Row, New York.

Morris, Desmond. 1985. Bodywatching: a field guide to human species. Jonathan Cape, London.

Morris, Henry. 1974. Scientific creationism. Creation-Life Publications, San Diego.

Morris, Robert. 1895. Lectures on appendicitis and notes on other subjects. G. P. Putman's and Sons, New York.

Morrison, Thomas (Editor). 1967. Human physiology. Holt, Rinehart and Winston, New York.

Moses, Robert A. (Editor). 1975. Adler's physiology of the eye: clinical application. C. V. Mosby, St. Louis.

Mullen, P. E. *et al.* 1979. Pineal 5-methoxytryptophol in man. *Psychoneural Endocrinology* 2:117-126.

Newman, Horatio Hackett. 1932. Evolution yesterday and today. Williams and Wilkins. Baltimore.

Nickel, Richard *et al.* 1986. The anatomy of the domestic animals. Vol. 1. The locomotory system of the domestic animals. Springer-Verlag, New York.

Norman, J. R., and P. H. Greenwood. 1975. A history of fishes. John Wiley, New York.

O'Brien, E. M. 1983. Do "vestigial organs" demand evolution? Edited by G. Howe. *Origins Research* 6(2):2.

Ouweneel, William J. 1975. Homeotic mutants and evolution. *Creation Research Society Quarterly* 12:141-154.

Ozer, H. and B. H. Waksman. 1970. Appendix and gamma-M antibody formation. IV. synergism of appendix and bone marrow cells in early antibody response to sheep erythrocytes. *The Journal of Immunology* 105:791-792.

Pansky, Ben. 1975. Dynamic anatomy and physiology. Macmillan Publishing, New York.

Parker, George. 1928. Vestigial organs, In: Creation by evolution, edited by Frances Mason. Macmillan, New York.

Pasewaldt, G. 1888. Experimentelle und histologische unterschungen uber die kompensatorische hypertrophe der ovarien (Dissertation), Bonn, Germany.

Pinchot, Roy. 1985. The skelton: fantastic framework. Torstar Books, New York.

Pittman, Tom. 1983. Coding theory and "vestigial" organs: a testable prediction from design. *Origins Research* 6(2):3 ff.

Pittman, Tom. 1984. Vestigial organs revisited. Edited by G. Howe. *Origins Research* 7(2):1 ff.

Pittman, Tom. 1989. Correspondence and conversation with Howe.

Prout, T. 1964. Observations on structural reduction in evolution. *American Naturalists* 98:239-249.

Pryor, Herbert (Editor). 1966. Keep your appendix. *Science Digest*. June, pp. 31-32.

Raven, Peter and George Johnson. 1988. Understanding biology. Times Mirror Mosby, St. Louis.

Redfern, P. H., I. C. Cambell, J. A. Davies and K. F. Martin (Editors). 1985. Circadian rhythms in the central nervous system. VCH Publishers, Deerfield Beach, FL.

Reiter, Russel J. 1977. The pineal-1977. The Eden Press, Montreal.

Relkin, Richard. 1976. The pineal-1976. The Eden Press, Montreal.

ReMine, W. 1971. Vestigial organs reassessed by evolutionists. *Bible Science Newsletter* 9(11):7.

ReMine, W. and J.M.K. (Anonymous) 1982. Child recently born with a tail? *Bible Science Newsletter (Five Minutes* insert) 20(8):8.

Reno, Cora. 1953. Evolution: fact or theory, Moody Press, Chicago. Many of the concepts expressed in this book are repeated with revision in her 1970 book.

Reno, Cora A. 1970. Evolution on trial. Moody Press. Chicago.

Rensch, Bernhard. 1959. Evolution above the species level. Columbia University Press, New York.

Ribbert, H. 1894. Beitrage zur kompensatorischen hypertrophie und zur regernation. *Archiv fur Entwiehlung Mechaniker* 1:69-90.

Richmond, Olney. 1896. Evolutionism. Temple Publishing, Chicago.

Ridgway, Sam H. 1972. Mammals of the sea. Charles C. Thomas, Springfield, IL.

Rigter, H. 1975. Plasma corticosterone levels as an index of ACTH induced attentuation of amnesia. *Behavioral Biology* 15:207-211.

Rijsbosch, J. K. C. 1960. Tail formation in man. *The Netherlands Journal of Surgery* 12:211-219.

Romer, Alfred. 1955. The vertebrate body. W. B. Saunders, Philadelphia.

Romer, Alfred Sherwood and Thomas S. Parsons. 1986. The vertebrate body. Sixth edition. Saunders College Publishing. Phildelphia.

Romero, Jorge and Julius Axelrod. 1974. Pineal B-adrenergic receptor: diurnal variation in sensitivity. *Science* 184:1091-1092.

Rusch, Wilbert. 1967. Analysis of so-called evidences of evolution. In: Why not creation? Edited by W.E. Lammerts. Creation Research Society Books, Kansas City, MO.

Rusch, Wilbert H., Sr. 1969. Ontogeny recapitulates phylogeny. *Creation Research Society Quarterly* 6:27-34.

Scadding, S. R. 1983. Do vestigial organs provide evidence for evolution? *Origins Research* 6(2):4-6. This paper was originally published in *Evolutionary Theory* 5:173-176, 1981.

Scheer, Bradley. 1965. Animal physiology. John Wiley, New York.

Scheffer, Victor B. 1976. A natural history of marine mammals. Charles Scribner's, New York.

Scheving, Lawrence E., Franz Habert and John Pauley (Editors). 1974. Chronobiology. Igaku Shoin, Tokyo.

Schmidek, Henry H. (Editor). 1977. Pineal tumors. Mason Publishing USA, New York.

Schoenfeld, R. I. 1971. Melatonin: effect on punished and nonpunished operant behavior of the pigeon. *Science* 171:1260.

Schultz, Leonard P. 1948. The ways of fishes. D. Van Nostrand, Princeton.

Shute, Evan. 1961. Flaws in the theory of evolution. The Temside Press, London, Canada. This work was republished by Craig Press, Nutley, NJ.

Sillman, E. I. 1985. Further comments on baleen fetal teeth and functions for yolk sacs. Edited by G. Howe. *Origins Research* 8(2):13-14.

Singer, Sam and Henry Hilgard. 1978. The biology of people. W. H. Freeman, San Francisco.

Sinnott, Edmund W. and Katherine S. Wilson. 1955. Botany: principles and problems. McGraw-Hill, New York.

Skoog, Gerald D. 1966. The topic of evolution in secondary school biology textbooks. *Science Education* 63:621-640.

Skoog, Gerald D. 1980. Textbook battle over creation. *Christian Century* 97:974-976.

Smith, Anthony. 1986. The body. Viking Penquin, New York.

Smyth, H. Rucker. 1962. Amphibians and their ways. Macmillan, New York.

Smythe, R. H. 1967. The horse: structure and movement. J. A. Allen, London.

Snyder, Solomon, Julius Axelrod and Mark Zweig. 1967. Circadian rhythm in the serotonin content of the rat pineal gland: regulating factors. *Journal of Pharmacology and Experimental Therapeutics.* 158:206-213.

Steele, E. J. 1981. Somatic selection and adaptive evolution: on the inheritance of acquired characteristics. University of Chicago Press, Chicago.

Stibbe, Philip. 1927. A comparative study of the nictitating membane of birds and mammals. *Journal of Anatomy* 163:159-176.

Stine, Gerald J. 1989. The new human genetics. W. C. Brown, Dubuque, IA.

Storer, Tracy and Robert L. Usinger. 1977. Elements of zoology. McGraw-Hill, New York.

Straus, William. 1947. Review of up from the ape. *Quarterly Review of Biology* 22:148-149.

Sussdorf, Dieter H. 1959. Quantitative changes in the white and red pulp of the spleen during hemolysin formation in X-irradiated and nonirradiated rabbits. *Journal of Infectious Diseases* 105:238-252.

Sussdorf, Dieter H. 1960. Repopulation of the spleen of X-irradiated rabbits by tritium-labeled lymphoid cells of the shielded appendix. *Journal of Infectious Diseases* 107:108-114.

Sussdorf, Dieter H. 1962. Partial body irridation and antibody response. In: The effects of ionizing radiation on immune processes. Edited by Charles Leone. Gordon and Breach Science, New York.

Sussdorf, Dieter H. 1974. Plague-forming cells in rabbits, following stimulation of the appendix with sheep erythrocytes. *Immunology* 27:305-310.

Tatina, Robert 1989. South Dakota high school biology teachers and the teaching of evolution and creationism. *The American Biology Teacher* 51:275-280.

Thomsen, Russel. 1974. The Bible book of medical wisdom. Old Tappan, NJ.

Thomson, Arthur. 1925. Concerning evolution. Yale University Press, New Haven, CT.

Thomson, Arthur. 1958. Riddles of science. Fawcett World Library, New York.

Thomson, K. S. 1988. Ontogeny and phylogeny recapitulated. *American Scientist* 76:273-275. For a creationist review of this article, see Lammerts, W. E. 1988. *Creation Research Society Quarterly* 25:147-148.

Turner, Donnell. 1966. General endocrinology. Fourth edition. W. B. Saunders, Philadelphia.

Vialleton, L. 1930. L'Origine des Etres Vivants. Librarie Plon, Paris.

Vianna. N. J., Petter Greenwald, and U. N. Davies. 1972. In: *Medical World News*, September 10:10.

Walker, Warren F. 1987. Functional anatomy of the vertebrates: an evolutionary perspective. Saunders College Publishing, Philadelphia.

Warrick, C. K. 1969. Anatomy and physiology for radiographers. Edward Arnold, London.

Warwick, Roger—see Eugene Wolff.

Watson, Lyall. 1981. Sea guide to whales of the world. E. P. Dutton, New York.

Way, Robert F. and Donald G. Lee. 1965. The anatomy of the horse. J. B. Lippincott, New York.

Webb, Norman and W. F. Vinal. 1934. Subject matter topics in biology courses of study. *School Science and Mathematics* 34:829-840.

Weichert, Charles. 1970. The anatomy of the chordate. McGraw-Hill, New York.

Weichert, Charles and William Presch. 1975. Elements of chordate anatomy. Fourth edition. McGraw-Hill, New York.

Weischnitzer, Saul. 1978. Outline of human anatomy. University Park Press, Baltimore.

Wetterberg, Lennert, Edward Geller and Arthur Yuwiler. 1970. Harderian gland: an extraretinal photoreceptor influencing the pineal gland in neonatal rats? *Science* 167:884-885.

Wiedersheim, Robert. 1895. The structure of man: an index to his past history. Translated by H. and M. Bernard. Macmillan, London.

Wilder-Smith, A. E. 1968. Man's origins, man's destiny. Harold Shaw, Wheaton, IL.

Wilder-Smith, A. E. 1979. Letter to J. Bergman.

Williams, Emmett L. (Editor). 1981. Thermodynamics and the development of order. Creation Research Society Books, Kansas City, MO.

Williams, John Gary. 1970. The other side of evolution. Williams Brothers Publishers, LaVernge, TN.

Wilson, Carl L. and Walter E. Loomis. 1957. Botany. Revised edition. Holt, Rinehart and Winston, New York.

Wolff, Eugene. (Revised by Robert Warwick). 1976. Anatomy of the eye and orbit. Seventh edition. W. B. Saunders, Philadelphia.

Wolfrom, Glen. 1989. Personal communication with Howe.

Wolstenholme, G. E. W. and Ruth Porter. 1966. The thymus: experimental and clinical studies. Little Brown, Boston.

Wurtman, Richard, Julius Axelrod and Douglas Kelley. 1968. The pineal. Academic Press, New York.

Yablokov, A. V. 1974. Variability of mammals. Amerind Publishing, New Delhi. Translated from the Russian by Jayant Honmode.

Yolles, Stanley. 1966. The pineal gland. *Today's Health* 44(3):76-79.

Young, J. Z. 1962. The life of vertebrates. Second edition. Oxford University Press, Oxford.

Zimmerman, Paul A. (Editor). 1959. Darwin evolution and creation. Concordia Publishing House, St. Louis.

Other books available from
Creation Research Society Books
P.O. Box 8263 • St. Joseph, MO 64508-8263
(catalog available)

Scientific Studies in Special Creation, edited by Walter E. Lammerts, Ph.D.

Speak to the Earth, edited by George F. Howe, Ph.D.

Thermodynamics and the Development of Order, edited by Emmett L. Williams, Ph.D.

Did Charles Darwin Become a Christian? by Wilbert H. Rusch, Sr., M.S., LL.D and John W. Klotz, Ph.D.

Creationist Rearch (1964-1980), by Duane T. Gish, Ph.D.

Vestigial Organs Are Fully Functional, by Jerry Bergman, Ph.D. and George F. Howe, Ph.D.

Origins: What Is at Stake? by Wilbert H. Rusch, Sr., M.S., LL.D.

Astronomy and Creation, by Donald B. DeYoung, Ph.D.

Ancient Ice Ages or Gigantic Submarine Landslides? by Michael J. Oard, M.S.

Physical Science and Creation, by Donald B. DeYoung, Ph.D.

Design and Origins in Astronomy, edited by George Mulfinger, M.S.

(continues, next page)

(continued from page 98)

Design and Origin in Astronomy, Volume 2, edited by Don B. DeYoung, Ph.D. and Emmett L. Williams, Ph.D.

Field Studies in Catastrophic Geology, by Carl R. Froede, Jr., P.G.

The North American Midcontinent Rift System, by John K. Reed, Ph.D.

The Human Body: An Intelligent Design, by Alan L. Gillen, Ed.D., Frank J. Sherwin III, M.A., and Alan Knowles, M.S.

Plate Tectonics: A Different View, edited by John K. Reed, Ph.D.

Natural History in the Christian Worldview, by John K. Reed, Ph.D.

Science and Creation, by Wayne Frair, Ph.D.

Biology and Creation, by Wayne Frair, Ph.D.

For more information about the
Creation Research Society and a subscription
to the *Creation Research Society Quarterly,* contact:
Membership Secretary
Creation Research Society
P.O. Box 8263
St. Joseph, MO 64508-8263
www.creationresearch.org
E-mail: contact@creationresearch.org